How to Do *Everything* with Your

Zire Handheld

I0002782

Dave Johnson
Rick Broida

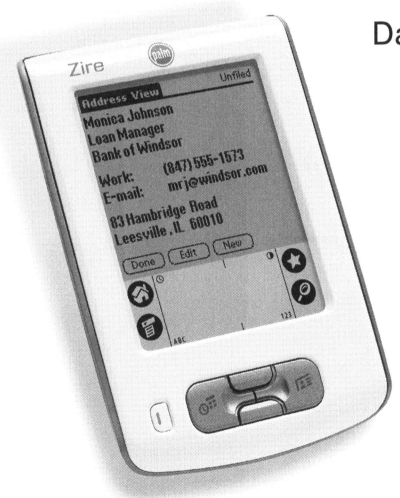

McGraw-Hill/Osborne

New York   Chicago   San Francisco
Lisbon   London   Madrid   Mexico City
Milan   New Delhi   San Juan
Seoul   Singapore   Sydney   Toronto

McGraw-Hill/Osborne
2600 Tenth Street
Berkeley, California 94710
U.S.A.

To arrange bulk purchase discounts for sales promotions, premiums, or fund-raisers, please contact **McGraw-Hill**/Osborne at the above address. For information on translations or book distributors outside the U.S.A., please see the International Contact Information page immediately following the index of this book.

How To Do Everything with Your Zire Handheld

1234567890 FGR FGR 019876543

ISBN 0-07-222930-6

Publisher	Brandon A. Nordin
Vice President & Associate Publisher	Scott Rogers
Executive Acquisitions Editor	Jane Brownlow
Project Editor	Elizabeth Seymour
Acquisitions Coordinator	Tana Allen
Technical Editor	Denny Atkin
Copy Editor	Dennis Weaver
Proofreader	Paul Medoff
Indexer	Robert J. Richardson
Computer Designers	Carie Abrew, John Patrus
Illustrators	Michael Mueller, Lyssa Wald
Series Design	Mickey Galicia
Cover Series Design	Dodie Shoemaker

This book was composed with Corel VENTURA™ Publisher.

About the Authors

Dave Johnson is the editor of Handheld Computing Mobility magazine; he also writes about digital photography for PC World magazine. In addition, he's the author of two dozen books including *Build Your Own Combat Robot, How to Do Everything with Your Digital Camera, How to Do Everything with MP3 and Digital Music* (written with Rick Broida), and *How to Use Digital Video.* His short story for early readers, *The Wild Cookie*, has been transformed into an interactive storybook on CD-ROM. In his spare time, Dave is a scuba instructor and wildlife photographer.

Rick Broida has written about computers and technology for more than a decade. A regular contributor to CNET and *Computer Shopper*, he specializes in mobile technology. In 1997, recognizing the unparalleled popularity of Palm handhelds and the need for a printed resource for users, he founded *Handheld Computing* (formerly *Tap Magazine*). He currently serves as editor of that magazine, which now includes all handheld platforms and devices. Rick also provides handheld-computing training seminars for corporate users and educators. He lives in Michigan with his wife and two children.

About the Technical Editor

Denny Atkin has been writing about technology since 1987, and about handheld computers since the Newton's release in 1993. After working with such pioneering technology magazines as *Compute!* and *Omni*, he's now editorial director of *Handheld Computing* and *Mobility Magazine*. Atkin lives with his wife, son, and giant Maine Coon cat in Vermont, a state where PDAs are nearly as popular as maple syrup.

Contents

Acknowledgments

This book was great fun to write, due in no small part to the great team at Osborne. Our thanks as always to Jane Brownlow, Tana Allen, Elizabeth Seymour, and Lyssa Wald. We'd especially like to thank tech editor Denny Atkin, who corrected the wildly inaccurate things we wrote.

Rick would also like to think Dave for staying on his meds long enough to write semi-lucid chapters. See, pal? Modern medicine works!

Dave would like to applaud Rick for finally getting his equivalency diploma—and just months before completing his sentence. Way to go, dude! Don't forget: you can keep reading even now that you no longer have access to the prison library.

Finally, thanks as always to our amazingly supportive families, who give us the time and space we need to get the work done, without so much as a single complaint.

Introduction

Zire handhelds are such neat little devices that any book about them runs the risk of reading like a promotional brochure. We've written thousands of pages about the Windows platform, and half of it always seems to be apologetic. "Computer locked up again? You need to reboot and send $94 in cash to Microsoft. . . ." Books about computers are often more about getting it to work in the first place or explaining why it doesn't work right than about telling you what you can actually accomplish.

Not the Zire, though. It's one of the most forgiving, user-friendly, and non-crashable computers ever created. And because it suffers from so few technical glitches, we were able to devote this book to work and play—accomplishing stuff while making your life more fun and efficient.

The book starts at the beginning (unlike those that start around, say, the midway point). First, we give you some of the history of handheld computers like the Zire. From there, you get a guided tour of your Zire and the accompanying desktop software. We teach you to navigate the core software, to input data, and to share information with your PC as well as other handheld devices.

Next, we show you the Zire's core applications and then tell you stuff you'd never think of—like how to get the most out of your Zire when you go on a business trip. Think your new handheld can't take the place of a laptop computer? Think again (and read Chapter 11).

The remainder of the book goes "beyond the box," and that's where things really get interesting. Read those chapters and you'll learn how to download Web pages to your Zire, manage your finances, track your stocks, and balance your checkbook. We also delve into the arts, with chapters on painting pictures and playing music. You might not think there's a lot to say about playing games, but a whole world of entertainment awaits you—and we show you how to tap into it (pun intended). In fact, you might throw away your Game Boy after reading Chapter 12. And, yes, we said people rarely have trouble with their Zires, but it does happen occasionally. We have that covered as well.

We wrote this book so you could sit down and read it through like a novel. But if you're looking for specific information, we made it easy to find. Plus, you can find special elements to help you get the most out of the book:

- **How to…**   These special boxes explain, in a nutshell, how to accomplish key tasks. Read them to discover key points covered in each chapter.

- **Notes**   These provide extra information that's often very important to gain understanding of a particular topic.

- **Tips**   These tell you how to do something smarter or faster.

- **Sidebars**   Here we address related—and, sometimes, unrelated—topics. Sidebars can be pretty interesting, if only to see us bicker like an old married couple.

Can't get enough of our witty banter? See the back page of Handheld Computing Magazine, where we continue our lively Head2Head column. You can also send questions and comments to us at *dave@bydavejohnson.com* and *rick@broida.com*. Thanks, and enjoy reading the book!

Welcome to Zire

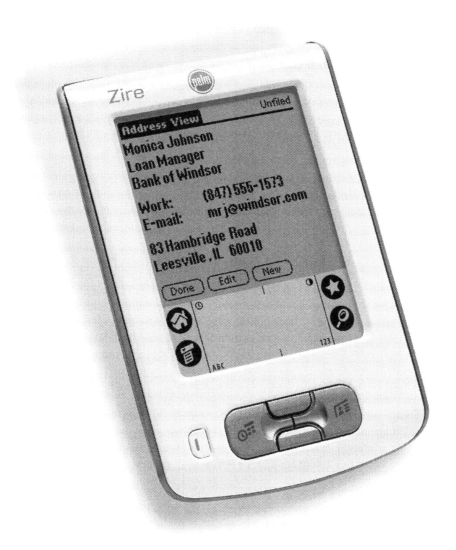

Stephen King novels. A thousand names and addresses. MapQuest driving directions. Your entire appointment calendar. A dozen great Solitaire games. A full-featured financial calculator.

All in your pocket.

It sounds like technology you might see on an episode of *Star Trek*, but you can have it right here in the 21st century. Thanks to remarkable strides in handheld computing, every item listed above can be stored in a single device—a Palm Zire handheld PC. And that's just the tip of the iceberg. These amazing devices let you jot notes in digital ink, open and edit Word and Excel files, wirelessly beam data to other handhelds (and receive data on yours), and a lot more.

In the pages and chapters to come, you'll learn the history of handheld PCs like the Zire, the differences between the Zire and other Palm models, and, of course, everything you need to know about using your Zire.

A Brief History of Handhelds

It all started with a block of wood. In 1994, Jeff Hawkins, founder of a little-known company called Palm Computing, envisioned a pocket-sized computer that would organize calendars and contacts, and maybe let travelers retrieve their e-mail from the road. This idea of a "personal digital assistant," or PDA, was by no means new, but previous attempts—like Apple's highly publicized Newton MessagePad—had failed to catch on with consumers.

Hawkins knew he'd have a tough time selling the concept, so he decided to convince himself before trying to convince investors. His device would be roughly the size of a deck of cards—much smaller and lighter than the Newton—and would therefore fit in a shirt pocket. But would it be practical even at that size? Would it be comfortable to carry around? Hawkins decided to find out. Before a single piece of plastic was molded, before a single circuit board was designed, the Palm Computing Pilot existed solely as a block of wood.

Hawkins cut a piece of balsa wood to the size he'd envisioned for his handheld device, put it in his shirt pocket, and left it there—for several months. He even took it out from time to time and pretended to take notes, just to see if the size and shape felt right. Though he quickly came to realize that such a form factor made perfect sense, doors slammed whenever he showed the "product" to potential investors. "The handheld market is dead," was the mantra at the time.

Fortunately, modem maker U.S. Robotics didn't think so and liked the idea of the Pilot so much that it bought Palm Computing outright. In March, 1996, the company unveiled the Pilot 1000, and the rest is history.

Flash forward seven years. The Pilot—which would eventually be renamed PalmPilot and then just Palm—had become the fastest growing computer platform in history, reaching the million-sold mark faster than the IBM PC or Apple Macintosh. In the interim, U.S. Robotics had been assimilated into networking giant 3Com, and Palm, Inc., along with it. The Palm line had grown to include a variety of models, and companies like Handspring, IBM, and Sony had adopted the Palm operating system for their own handheld devices.

Today, the *Palm platform* (an umbrella term used to describe not only the actual hardware, but the operating system that drives it) is dominant in the explosive handheld market. The Zire falls under that umbrella. It's a handheld PC that runs the Palm Operating System (OS)—the same OS used in other handhelds made by Palm, Sony, and other companies.

What's an Operating System?

Windows is an operating system. Mac OS X is an operating system. The core software that drives
any computer is an operating system. Hence, when we refer to the Zire's Palm OS, we're talking
about the software that's built right into the device—the brains behind the brawn. The Palm OS
itself not only controls the Zire's fundamental operations, such as what happens when you press
a button or tap the screen, but also supplies the built-in applications (the address book, memo
pad, date book and so on—all of which we discuss in detail in later chapters).

You can see that a Zire looks quite a bit different from a Palm (see Figure 1-1), but on the
inside they're fundamentally the same. They both use the Palm Operating System, and therefore
operate in similar fashion and are capable of running almost all the same software.

What Makes Handheld PCs So Great?

Why all the fuss? What makes Palm OS devices like the Zire so special? To answer these questions,
we'll first need to look at what a handheld PC actually is. Put simply, it's a pocket-sized electronic
organizer that enables you to manage addresses, appointments, expenses, tasks, and memos. If
you've ever used a Franklin Planner or similar kind of paper-bound organizer, you get the idea.

However, because a handheld PC is electronic, there's no paper or ink involved. Instead,
you write directly on the device's screen using a small plastic stylus that takes the place of a pen.
A key advantage here, of course, is that you're able to store all of your important personal and
business information on a device that's much small and lighter than a paper planner.

FIGURE 1-1   Palm OS handhelds don't all look the same, and in fact can look quite different,
but they all use the same core operating system.

What's the Difference Between a Zire and a Palm?

It's easy to get confused between "Palm," "Zire," "Palm OS," and other terms we use frequently in this book. Therefore, here's a lexicon to help you understand the basic terminology.

- **Handheld PC** A portable, pocket-sized computer like the Palm m505, Palm Zire, and Sony Clié.

- **Operating system** The core software that makes a handheld PC function.

- **Palm, Inc.** The company that makes handheld PCs that run the Palm Operating System (OS).

- **Palm OS** The operating system used in Palm, Handspring, Sony, and many other handheld PCs.

- **Palm Powered** Denotes a handheld PC that runs the Palm OS. "Palm Powered" is a registered trademark of Palm, Inc.

- **PalmSource** The division of Palm, Inc., responsible for developing the Palm OS.

- **PDA** Short for Personal Digital Assistant, a generic term used to describe any handheld PC.

- **Pocket PC** Microsoft's Windows-like operating system for handheld PCs. Found in devices from Dell, Hewlett-Packard, Toshiba, and other vendors.

What's more, you can easily share that information with your Windows-based or Macintosh computer. Handheld PCs are not self-contained: they can *synchronize* with a desktop computer and keep information current on both sides. This is an important advantage, as it effectively turns your handheld into an extension of the computer you use every day. Changes and additions made to your desktop data are reflected in the device and vice versa (see Figure 1-2).

Saying that a Zire is an extension of your PC is only a half-truth: in reality, it has evolved into a computer in its own right. That's because it is capable of running additional software written by parties other than Palm, Inc., and those parties (known as software developers) number in the tens of thousands. There are literally thousands of programs and data files that extend your Zire's capabilities, from spreadsheet managers and expense trackers to electronic-book readers and word processors.

NOTE *While the first several chapters of this book are devoted to the Zire's core capabilities—the things it can do right out of the box—the majority of it focuses on these "extended" capabilities: the things that have elevated the device from a basic electronic organizer to a full-fledged handheld PC.*

FIGURE 1-2   A Zire connects to a PC via a HotSync cable, which allows data to be synchronized on both devices.

Above all else, simplicity is a major key to the platform's success. The devices are amazingly easy to use, requiring no more than a few taps of the stylus to access your data and a little memorization to master the handwriting-recognition software. Most users, even those who have little or no computer experience (like Dave), find themselves tapping and writing productively within 20 minutes of opening the box.

Zire 101: The Basics

Whether you've just pried open the blister pack (that's the name used to describe the impossible-to-open packaging that contains the Zire and lots of other products these days) or you've been fiddling with your Zire for a month, it's good to have a basic understanding of its features and capabilities. (This is where we unintentionally sound like Palm salesmen, which we're not.)

- **Built-in software**   Right out of the box, the Zire includes all the software you need to manage appointments, addresses, tasks, memos, and expenses. It also includes a digital-ink scratchpad for doodles and quick notes. On Palm's software CD you'll find a couple of games, which must be installed separately. (More about that in Chapter 4.)

- **Handwriting recognition**   Your Zire can recognize your handwriting—sort of. Using built-in software called Graffiti, the Zire lets you write directly on the screen. This is one way to get names, addresses, and other information into the unit. Another is with a keyboard that pops up on the screen. A third is via your computer. The next few chapters tell you all about entering data and synchronizing with your PC.

■ **Rechargeable battery** Most first-generation Palm handhelds relied on AAA batteries, but the Zire has a built-in rechargeable battery. Once it's fully charged, it should last you upwards of a month before it needs charging again. And its AC adapter is small enough to toss in a backpack or purse, so it's easy to bring along when you travel.

■ **Memory** The Zire sports 2MB (megabytes) of memory. That probably doesn't sound like much, but it's enough to hold thousands of addresses, appointments, and other records—plus some third-party software.

■ **Synchronization** As noted earlier, your Zire can link to your computer for two-way synchronization. Better still, it supports both Windows- and Macintosh-based PCs and can synchronize with its own special software (called Palm Desktop, which is included) or Microsoft Outlook. See Chapter 3 for information on connecting your Zire to your computer and setting up its synchronization software.

Top 10 Reasons to Own a Zire

You'll see boxes like this one throughout the book. Why? Mostly because Dave and Rick rarely agree about anything—and they feel a need to share with the world both their disagreements and those rare moments when they actually get along.

Rick: Sure, it's amazingly inexpensive and cute as a bug, but those aren't the very best reasons to own a Zire. With apologies to David Letterman, here they are.

10. Gives you a perfect pickup line at trade shows: "Hey, why don't we get together and HotSync?"

9. You can play Bejeweled during boring board meetings and no one will ever know.

8. Looks enough like Captain Kirk's communicator to let you live out your *Star Trek* fantasies.

7. You can read Monica Lewinsky's biography and no one will ever know.

6. People will be impressed as hell when you show off the MapQuest directions you downloaded to it.

Dave:

5. Cool, it's something new to lose (or at least to leave in your pocket when you do laundry)!

4. Finally, a new excuse: "Yes, I wrote that marketing report, but I dropped it and it broke."

3. Makes you look like a spy.

2. It's smarter than your dog. Actually, that's also true of your houseplants and silverware.

1. If it doesn't use batteries, it's not worth having!

Chapter 2

Get to Know Your Zire

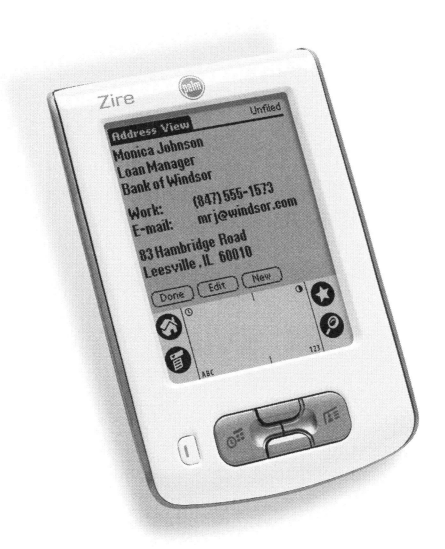

How to...

■ Identify the buttons on a Zire
■ Identify the infrared transmitter
■ Work with the screen and Graffiti area
■ Charge the batteries
■ Reset a Zire
■ Configure a Zire's preferences
■ Reset the screen digitizer
■ Work with the operating system
■ Check how much memory is left
■ Create and use shortcuts
■ Work with Palm Desktop

Okay, enough history—it's time to dive in and start having fun. In this chapter, we delve into the Zire hardware: the screen, buttons, handwriting area, and so on. If you read only one chapter from start to finish, make sure it's this one!

A Guided Tour of the Hardware

By now your Zire is no doubt out of the box and getting the once-over. You're seeing buttons, a screen, some little pictures, and a funny-looking piece of rubber. What is all this stuff? What does it do?

The Screen

A Zire screen is capable of displaying roughly 15 lines of text, each about 32 characters across. It can also display graphics with up to 16 shades of gray.

2

When you use a desktop computer, you use a mouse to navigate and a keyboard to enter data. With a Zire, you use a plastic-tipped stylus for both navigation and data entry. That's because the screen is, technically speaking, a *touchscreen,* meaning you interact with it by tapping it and writing on it. If you want to access, say, the Expense program, you tap the Expense icon that appears on the screen. If you want to record the price of the dinner you just ate, you write the numbers on the screen.

Many novice users think they have to double-tap the application icons, just like double-clicking with a mouse. Not true! A single tap is all you ever need when working with a Zire.

The Difference Between Tapping and Writing

Tapping the screen is the equivalent of clicking a mouse. You tap icons to launch programs, tap to access menus and select options in them, and tap to place your cursor in specific places. Writing on the screen is, of course, like putting a pen to paper. However, most writing you do on a Zire takes place in a specific area of the screen, which we discuss in the next section. When you're working in the Note Pad application, though, you can scribble anywhere on the screen, just as though it were a blank sheet of paper.

Don't press too hard with the stylus. The screen is fairly sensitive, and light pressure is all it takes to register a tap or stylus stroke. If you press too hard, you could wind up with a scratched screen—the bane of every Zire user.

The Graffiti Area

As you have no doubt noticed, the bottom portion of the screen looks a bit different. That big rectangular box flanked by two pairs of icons is called the *Graffiti area,* referring to the handwriting-recognition software that's a part of every Zire (and, for that matter, every handheld PC that has the Palm Operating System). Graffiti makes it possible to enter information using the stylus, but you can do so only within the confines of the Graffiti area (as seen in Figure 2-1).

You may have discovered a Graffiti cheat-sheet sticker among the materials that came with your handheld. However, the Palm OS has a built-in cheat sheet of its own. Just draw a line from anywhere in the Graffiti area all the way to the top of the screen. Presto—a diagram of all the Graffiti characters!

We tell you more about Graffiti—how to use it and alternatives to it—in Chapters 4 and 13.

What about those icons on either side and in the corners of the Graffiti area? They serve some important functions. We present an overview in the following sections.

The Applications Icon   Represented by a picture of a house and located to the left of the Graffiti area, the *Applications icon* is the one you'll tap more often than any other. From whatever

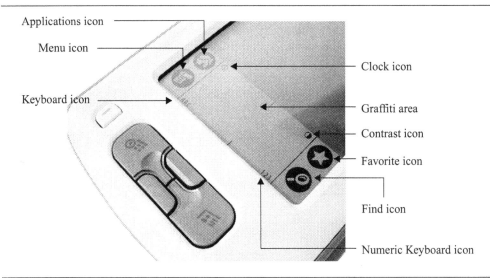

Applications icon
Menu icon
Keyboard icon
Clock icon
Graffiti area
Contrast icon
Favorite icon
Find icon
Numeric Keyboard icon

FIGURE 2-1 The Graffiti area is where you write data into your handheld and access various options like menus, the clock, and "home base."

program you're currently running, the Applications icon (see Figure 2-1) takes you back to the main screen—"home base," as it were (hence the house picture).

When you're using any program, tapping the Applications icon returns you to the main screen. When you're already viewing that screen, however, tapping the Applications icon cycles through the application categories, which we discuss later in this chapter.

The Menu Icon   The *Menu icon* (see Figure 2-1) gives you access to the drop-down menus that are part of the Palm Operating System. These menus vary somewhat from program to program insofar as the options they provide, but they're fairly consistent within the core Palm OS applications.

The Menu icon works like a toggle switch. If you accidentally tap it or simply want to make the drop-down menus go away, simply tap it again. In many applications, you can also tap the upper-left corner of the screen to access drop-down menus.

The Favorite Icon   Located to the right of the Graffiti area (see Figure 2-1), the *Favorite icon*—represented by a star—is used to load whatever program you choose, be it one of the built-in applications or a program you install yourself. By default, however, it activates the HotSync process, which you learn about in Chapters 3 and 4. Meanwhile, see the section titled "The Buttons" later in this chapter for information on changing the function of the Favorite icon.

NOTE *We strongly encourage you to experiment with almost every area of your Zire, but don't tap this icon unless you're ready to HotSync your Zire with your PC—meaning you've installed the necessary software, plugged in its USB cable (see Chapter 3), and so on. If you do accidentally press it, tap the Cancel button and wait for the HotSync process to abort before doing anything else.*

The Find Icon   Next, we come to the little magnifying glass in the lower-right corner. Because a Zire can store such vast amounts of information, and because sifting through all that information to find what you're looking for can be tedious, there's a handy little search feature called the *Find icon* (see Figure 2-1). We talk more about it in Chapter 9.

The Clock Icon   Represented by a little clock-like circle and located in the upper-left corner of the Graffiti area (see Figure 2-1), the *Clock icon* activates the Zire's built-in Clock program. When you tap it, the date and time appear briefly, and then you're returned to whatever screen you were viewing previously. It's like glancing at your wristwatch when you need to know the time. Learn more about the Clock program, including using it to set an alarm, in Chapter 9.

The Contrast Icon   Opposite the Clock icon, the *Contrast icon* (see Figure 2-1) activates an onscreen slider used to adjust screen contrast. Tap it, and then tap and hold your stylus on the slider tool. Move it left and right to see the effect it has on the screen; then find a setting that's comfortable for you and release the stylus. Tap Done, and you're done! You can access this tool at any time, from within any application, should the need arise.

The Keyboard Icon   In the lower-left corner of the Graffiti area, notice the little ABC (see Figure 2-1). When you tap this *Keyboard icon*, an onscreen keyboard appears, allowing you to "tap-type" instead of using Graffiti to enter data. Read all about this keyboard in Chapter 4, and alternatives to it in Chapter 13.

The Numeric Keyboard Icon   Opposite the ABC, notice the 123 (see Figure 2-1). This *Numeric Keyboard icon* brings up, natch, a numeric onscreen keyboard—used to input numbers and symbols. Find out more about it in Chapter 4.

The Buttons

Below the Graffiti area on every Zire, you can see four buttons grouped together and a fifth button to the left (see Figure 2-2). These serve some fairly important functions: to turn the device on and off, to instantly launch two of the core applications (Date Book and Address Book), and to scroll up and down in screens of data.

The Two Program Buttons

So you want to look up a number in your address book. You could turn on your Zire, tap the Applications button to get to the main screen, and then find and tap the Address button. There's a much faster way: simply press the Address button (see Figure 2-2), which is the large, right-hand button that looks like a Rolodex card. That serves the dual function of turning on the Zire *and* loading the Address Book program.

The same holds true for the Date Book button (see Figure 2-2)—press it to turn on the Zire and start the Date Book program. Of course, you're not limited to using these buttons when the Zire is off. You can use them at any time, whether the Zire is on or off, to quickly switch between these two commonly used core programs. Go ahead and try: push one, then the other, then the first one again, and see what happens. Pretty simple, huh?

The Scroll Buttons

Sandwiched between the two Program buttons, the *Scroll buttons* are used to cycle through multiple screens of data. If you're looking at a memo that's too long to fit on the screen in its entirety, you'd use the *Scroll down button* to move down to the next section—not unlike turning pages in a book. The *Scroll up button* simply moves you back a page.

NOTE   *In many programs, onscreen arrows serve the same function. Instead of having to press the Scroll buttons, you can simply tap the arrows with your stylus. This is largely a matter of personal preference: try both and decide which method you like better, or switch between them as the situation warrants. The Palm OS often gives you multiple ways to accomplish the same task.*

TIP   *When your Zire is off, pressing the Scroll up button has the same effect as tapping the Clock icon when the Zire is on: it makes the clock appear for a few seconds. After that, the Zire shuts off again.*

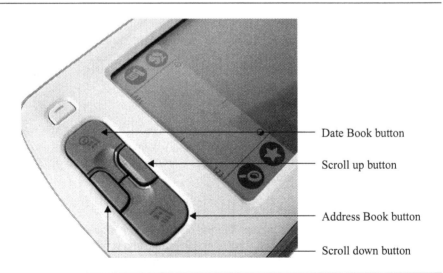

Date Book button

Scroll up button

Address Book button

Scroll down button

FIGURE 2-2   The Date Book, Address Book, and Scroll buttons

2

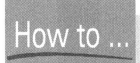 **Reprogram Your Zire's Buttons**

Want the Address Book button to load the Memo Pad program instead, or the Favorite icon to run your e-book application? You can reprogram the Zire's two Program buttons and Favorite icon to run any installed program. Just tap the Prefs icon and select Buttons from the drop-down list in the upper-right corner of the Preferences screen. Now assign your desired applications to the various buttons. If you change your mind later, just return to that screen and tap the Default button that appears there. It will restore all the buttons to their original settings.

The Power Button

You don't really need us to explain the *Power button* (see Figure 2-2), do you? Okay, push it to turn the Zire on. Push it again to turn the Zire off. Just so this paragraph doesn't turn out to be a total insult of your intelligence, we should mention that your Zire will automatically shut itself off after a certain period of inactivity. This helps preserve the battery. See the section titled "General" later in this chapter to learn how to change the auto-off setting.

The Back of the Zire

Flip your Zire over. Yes, it's pretty boring back there, but you should know about one important area: the Reset button. Every Zire has a little hole on the back that's used to reset the device. Hey, every computer crashes occasionally, and the Palm OS isn't entirely glitch-free. To reset a frozen Zire, push a paper clip or narrow pin briefly into the hole. (We talk more about resetting in the troubleshooting section in Chapter 15.)

The Infrared Port

At the top of the Zire there's a small, black-plastic window. Behind it lies the *infrared port,* also known as the *infrared transceiver* or *IR port.* It's used to wirelessly beam data from one Zire to another, and has a range of about five feet. You learn more about beaming in Chapter 4.

 *By holding down the Address Book button for two seconds, you can automatically beam your "business card" to another handheld user. In Chapter 6, you learn how to designate an address book record as your card.*

The Stylus

Last, but definitely not least, we come to the *stylus*. Every Zire has a small plastic pen tucked away inside. Under no circumstances should you ever use any kind of ink pen or metal tip on a Zire's screen. That's a sure way to create a scratch, and a scratched screen is a damaged screen.

TIP   *There's one exception. In a pinch, or if you just don't feel like extracting the stylus, you can use your fingernail for light taps on the screen.*

Using Your Zire for the First Time

Now that you're familiar with the Zire hardware, you're ready to start using it. This includes charging the device, working your way through the startup screens, and checking out the Graffiti tutorial.

Charging the Battery

Before you use the Zire for the first time, you must charge it completely using the included AC adapter. We know you're eager to start using it, but make sure you let it charge fully before going on to the next steps. It takes about four hours. On subsequent occasions, it will probably take less than an hour to fully charge the battery, and that's if it's fully drained. Usually you'll "top off" the charge by plugging it in for a few minutes each day, which is what we recommend.

The Welcome Screens

The very first time you turn on your Zire, you see a "welcome" screen that asks you to remove the stylus and tap anywhere to continue. You're about to undertake a one-time setup procedure that takes all of about 60 seconds. The two key tasks accomplished here are the calibration of the screen digitizer and the setting of the date and time.

Beyond the Box

Rick: Because the Zire uses the Palm Operating System, it's compatible with thousands of additional programs. I think the first acquisition for any Zire owner should be Palm Reader, a free e-book viewer that's available from Palm Digital Media (**www.palmdigitalmedia.com**). With it you can read free, public domain books downloaded from places like MemoWare (**www.memoware.com**), as well as commercial fiction and nonfiction purchased from Palm Digital Media. I'm reading Jonathan Franzen's *The Corrections* on my handheld, and loving it!

Dave: Actually, one of your best bets is AvantGo (**www.avantgo.com**), a free service that installs your favorite Web-based news and entertainment sites on your PDA at each HotSync. It's very cool to take the latest *New York Times* to lunch with you each day on your Zire, so this should absolutely be the first program you install.

What Is Digitizer Calibration?

Put simply, *digitizer calibration* is the process of teaching a Zire to accurately recognize taps on the screen. As you know, the screen responds to input from the stylus, and this calibration process simply ensures the precision of those responses. In a way, it's like fine-tuning a TV set.

NOTE   *Over time, you might discover your screen taps seem a little "off." For example, you have to tap a bit to the left of an arrow for the screen to register the tap. At this point, it's time to recalibrate the digitizer, which you can do in the Prefs menu. We tell you how later in this chapter.*

Setting the Date and Time

The last stage of the welcome process is setting the date and time (and choosing your country, if you live outside the United States). To set the time, you simply tap the box next to the words Set Time and then tap the up/down arrow keys to select the current time (don't forget to specify AM or PM). Tapping the box next to Set Date reveals a calendar. Again, a few strategic taps is all it takes to select today's date. (Be sure to choose the year first, then the month, then the day.) When you've done so, tap the Today button.

 *If you find yourself in a different time zone and need to change your Zire's clock, you needn't repeat the whole "welcome" process to do so. The date and time settings can be found in the Prefs menu, which we discuss later in this chapter.*

Getting to Know the Operating System

We aren't exaggerating when we say working with a Zire is roughly eight gazillion times easier than working with traditional computers. Though plenty powerful, Zires are just a lot less complicated. There's no confusing menu system to wade through, no accidentally forgetting to save your document. Here we've highlighted some of the fundamental—but still important—differences between a Zire and a PC:

■ When you turn on a PC, you have to wait a few minutes for it to boot up. When you turn on a Zire, it's ready to roll instantaneously. Same goes for shutting it off—just press the power button and the screen goes dark. There's no lengthy shutdown procedure.

■ On a PC, when you're done working with a program (say, your word processor), you must save your data before exiting that program. On a Zire, this isn't necessary. Data is retained at all times, even if you, say, switch to your to-do list while in the middle of writing a memo. When you return to Memo Pad, you find your document exactly as you left it. This holds true even if you turn the Zire off!

■ In that same vein, you don't "exit" a Zire program so much as switch to another one. This is a hard concept for seasoned computer users to grasp, as we've all been taught to shut down our software when we're done with it. There's no exit procedure on a Zire, and you'll never find that word in a drop-down menu. When you finish working in one program, you just tap the Applications button to return to home base or press one of the program buttons.

 *We strongly encourage experimentation. Whereas wandering too far off the beaten track in Windows can lead to disaster, it's virtually impossible to get "lost" using a Zire. So tap here, explore there, and just have fun checking things out. Because there's no risk of losing data or running too many programs at once (impossible in the Palm OS), you should have no fear of fouling anything up. Play!*

The Icons

Icons are, of course, little pictures used to represent things. In the case of the Palm OS, they're used largely to represent the installed programs. Thus, on the Applications screen, you see icons labeled Address, Calc, Date Book, and so on—and all you do is tap one to access that particular program.

2

 Say, didn't you just learn that pressing the Date Book button is the way to load Date Book? In the Palm OS, there are often multiple ways to accomplish the same task. In this case, you can load certain programs either by tapping their onscreen icons or using their hardware-button equivalents.

The Menus

As in most computers, *drop-down menus* are used to access program-specific options and settings. In most Palm programs, tapping the Menu button makes a small "menu bar" appear at the top of the screen. You navigate this bar using the stylus as you would a mouse, tapping each menu item to make its list of options drop down and tapping the option you want to access.

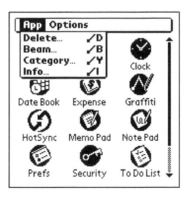

 There's another way to access menus. Instead of tapping the Menu button (which you can still do if you want), you merely have to tap the "title bar" at the top of the screen. In the Applications screen, for instance, you tap the clock in the upper-left corner. In Address Book, you tap the word "Address." This isn't unlike working with a PC, where you click the mouse near the top of the screen to pull down menus.

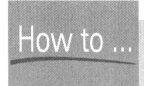 **Find Out How Much Memory Your Handheld Has Left**

As you start to add records and install new software on your Zire, you may wonder how to check the amount of memory that's available. From the Applications screen, tap Menu | App | Info. The screen that appears shows the total amount of memory on your device and how much of it is free. Notice, too, the other options that appear when you tap Menu | App. There's Delete (used to delete third-party programs), Beam (used to beam third-party programs), and Category (used to organize your programs into categories—see the next section).

The Applications Screen

On a Zire, *home base* is the Applications screen, which displays the icons for all the installed programs. (It also shows you the time and a battery gauge, as the following illustrates.)

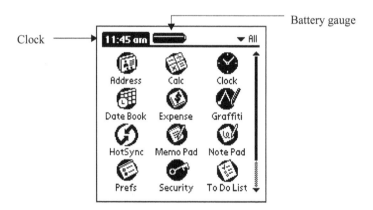

In the upper-right corner of the screen, you'll also notice a small arrow next to the word "All." What this means is the Applications screen is currently showing you all of the installed programs. If you tap the arrow, you see a list of categories (see Figure 2–3) into which you can group your programs.

Why Use Categories?

The use of categories is entirely optional. They're intended solely to help you keep your applications organized. See, as you install more software, you wind up with more icons. Right out of the box, a Zire has only about a dozen of them—a manageable number. But, suppose you install a few games and a mail program and an e-book reader. Now things are getting a little cluttered, icon-wise.

2

FIGURE 2-3   In the Applications screen, categories can be used to organize your programs.

Categories offer you a way to minimize the clutter. As you saw in the drop-down list, the Zire comes with a number of categories already created. You can use them if you want or create your own.

How to Create and Modify Categories   Look again at the drop-down list in the upper-right corner of the Applications screen (see Figure 2–3). Notice the last option: Edit Categories. Tapping this takes you to a screen where you can add, rename, and delete categories. To rename or delete one, first select it by tapping it with the stylus (you see it becomes highlighted). Then, tap the appropriate button.

To create a new category, tap the New button and then write in the desired name. That's all there is to it!

How to Assign Programs to Categories   Once you tailor the categories to your liking, you must next assign your programs to them. This isn't difficult, but it may take you a few tedious minutes to complete. Here's how:

1. In the Applications screen, tap the Menu button and select Category.

2. Identify any one program you want to assign (you may have to scroll down the list, which you can do by using on the onscreen arrows or scroll bar, or the scroll buttons), then tap the little arrow next to it.

3. The list of categories appears. Pick one by tapping it.

4. Repeat the procedure for the other programs you want to assign.

5. Tap Done to return to the Applications screen.

Now, when you tap the category arrow in the corner and select one, you see that all your reassigned icons have been placed in the respective screens.

 *One way to change the displayed category is to tap the aforementioned arrow. However, there's a quicker way: if you tap the Applications icon repeatedly, the Zire cycles through the categories that have programs assigned to them. Again, the Palm OS offers us two ways to accomplish the same goal.*

Setting Zire Preferences

What would a computer be without a control panel where you can tweak the settings and customize the machine? The Palm OS has one, called *Prefs*. Find the Prefs icon in the Applications screen, tap it, and meet us at the next paragraph.

Divided into several different sections (all of them accessible by tapping the arrow in the upper-right corner of the screen), Prefs is the place to reset your Zire's digitizer, change the date and time, and more. In listed order, here's the scoop on each individual Pref.

Buttons

As we explained earlier, the two Program buttons below the screen are used to quick-launch Date Book and Address Book. However, it is possible to reassign these buttons (and the Favorite icon) to launch other programs instead.

After selecting Buttons from the drop-down menu in the Prefs screen, you see an icon that corresponds to each button. All you do to change the function of any given button is tap the little arrow next to it and select the desired application. The buttons can launch any installed application—you're not limited to just the core Zire apps.

2

Notice, too, the two options at the bottom of the Buttons screen. *Default* restores the button assignments to their original settings. *Pen* lets you choose what happens when you drag the tip of your stylus from the Graffiti area to the top of the screen. (This action can be made to load the built-in Graffiti help screens, invoke the onscreen keyboard, or even beam a record.)

Connection

You'll probably never need to do anything in the *Connection* screen, which is where you can modify HotSync settings.

Date & Time

Flying into another time zone? Hit this screen to change your handheld's internal clock (an important thing to remember so you don't miss your alarms!). You can also change the date if necessary, and set the Zire to automatically adjust for Daylight Saving.

Digitizer

Noticing a little "drift" in your stylus taps? You tap someplace, but it doesn't quite register, or it registers in the *wrong* place? It may be time to reset your screen's digitizer. You should do so the moment you notice a problem; the worse the drift gets, the harder it may be to get to this screen. All you do is select Digitizer from the menu and follow the instructions.

Digitizer drift does occur over time, but if it becomes a frequent occurrence, it could point to a hardware problem. If your Zire is still under warranty, contact customer service to see if a replacement is warranted.

Formats

Few users need to spend much time in the *Formats* screen, where you can change the way dates, times, and numbers are displayed. You can also specify whether you want the calendar week to start on Sunday (the default) or Monday.

General

Probably the most frequently visited of the Prefs screens, *General* contains the following settings:

- **Auto-off After** To help preserve battery life, your handheld will turn itself off after a designated period of inactivity. Here you can set the interval, from 30 seconds to 3 minutes. The lower you set it, the better your battery life will be.

- **On While Charging** When this box is checked, your handheld will remain on while it's connected to the AC adapter. This can be handy if you spend a lot of time at your desk and frequently need to consult your handheld for addresses, schedules, and so forth.

- ■ **System Sound**   Adjusts the volume for various system sounds (like beeps, HotSync tones, and so forth). If you want your handheld to be silent, set this to Off.
- ■ **Alarm Sound**   Adjusts the volume for alarms.
- ■ **Game Sound**   Adjusts the volume for games.
- ■ **Beam Receive**   If this is off, you won't be able to receive programs and data beamed from other handhelds. However, keeping it off until you need it can help conserve power. Just *remember* that it's off so you don't pull your hair out trying to figure out why you can't receive a beam.

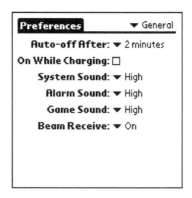

Network

Another screen you probably won't ever need to visit, the slightly misnamed *Network* is where you enter the relevant information about your Internet service provider (ISP), if you're using a modem or mobile phone to dial into it. A handful of major ISPs are already listed in the Service menu, but you still need to provide your account username and password, plus the phone number for the ISP. The *Details* button takes you to a screen with some advanced Internet settings, while *Connect* tells the modem to go ahead and dial in.

Owner

In the tragic event that you lose your Zire, you'd probably be very grateful to have it returned. The Owner screen is where you can put your name and contact information (address, phone number, e-mail address—whatever you're comfortable with). Then, if you use the Palm Operating System's security features (which we detail in Chapter 9) to "lock" the device when you turn it off, the information on the Owner screen is displayed when the unit is turned on again. Thus, if someone happens to find your handheld, they'll know how to return it to you, but won't have access to all your data. Smart!

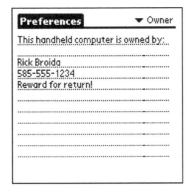

TIP   *Here's an even better way to retrieve a lost Zire: slap on a Boomerangit sticker. (There may be one in your Zire box.) Whoever finds your handheld simply needs to call a toll-free number or visit a Web site to arrange its return. Get more information on this great service at **www.boomerangit.com**.*

ShortCuts

Next, we come to *ShortCuts,* a tool designed to expedite the entry of often-used words and phrases. Let's say you're a Star Fleet engineer, and you use your Zire to keep track of your repair duties. The phrase "holodeck emitter malfunction" comes up quite a bit—but do you really have to write it out every time? What if you could just write "hem" instead, and have the words magically appear? That's the beauty of shortcuts.

As you see when you reach the ShortCuts screen, a handful of the little time savers have already been created. There's one each for your daily meals, one for "meeting," and even a couple of date and time stamps (used to quickly insert the date and time, natch). Let's walk through the process of creating and using a new shortcut:

1. Tap the New button.

2. In the ShortCut Name field, write the abbreviation you want to use for this particular shortcut. As an example, let's use "bm" for "Buy milk."

3. Tap the first line in the ShortCut Text field to move your cursor there. Now, enter the text you want to appear when you invoke the shortcut (in this case, "Buy milk").

4. Tap OK. Now, let's invoke the new shortcut. Press the To Do button to launch the To Do List and then tap New to create a new task.

5. To invoke this or any other shortcut (in any application, be it Date Book, Memo Pad or whatever), you must first write the shortcut stroke in the Graffiti area. This lets Graffiti know you're about to enter the abbreviation for a shortcut. The stroke looks like a cursive, lowercase letter *l* (see our Graffiti guide in Chapter 4). After you make the stroke, you see it appear next to your cursor. Now enter the letter *b,* then the letter *m.* Presto! The words "Buy milk" magically appear.

An Introduction to Palm Desktop

So far, we've talked mostly about the Zire itself: the hardware, the operating system, and the basic setup procedures and considerations. There's one area left to cover before you venture into real-world Zire use: the Palm Desktop.

What Is Palm Desktop?

Wondrous as a Zire is in its own right, what makes it even more special is its capability to synchronize with your computer. This means all the data entered into your Zire is copied to your PC, and vice versa. The software that fields all this data on the computer side is *Palm Desktop*. (If you use Microsoft Outlook or another contact manager, you needn't use Palm Desktop at all. More on that in the next section.)

Viewed in a vacuum, Palm Desktop resembles traditional personal information management (PIM) or contact-management software. It effectively replicates all the core functionality of the Palm OS, providing you with a phone list, appointment calendar, to-do list, and memo pad (see the following illustrations).

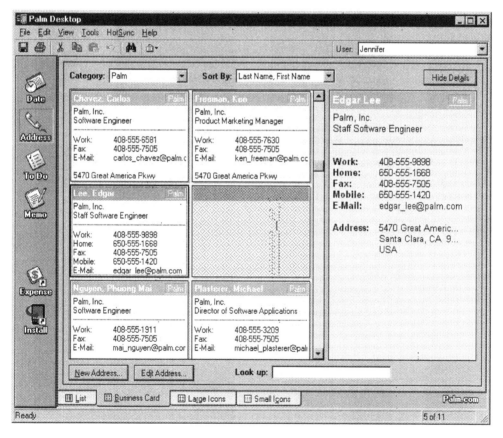

If you've never used such software before, you'll no doubt find Palm Desktop an invaluable addition, as it helps keep you organized at home or in the office (whereas a Zire keeps you organized while traveling).

A Word About Synchronization

What happens when you synchronize your Zire with your PC? In a nutshell, three things:

- Any new entries made on your Zire are added to Palm Desktop.
- Any new entries made in Palm Desktop are added to your Zire.
- Any existing records modified in one place (the Zire, for example) are modified in the other (the desktop, same example), the newest changes taking precedence.

Therefore, synchronizing regularly assures your information is kept current, both in your Zire and in Palm Desktop.

Already entrenched in Microsoft Outlook? All Zires come with software—Chapura PocketMirror—that allows direct synchronization with Outlook (bypassing Palm Desktop). If you have a different contact manager (such as Lotus Notes), you may need to upgrade to a different sync program, like Puma's IntelliSync.

The Differences Between the Windows and Macintosh Versions

While functionally similar, the Windows and Macintosh versions of Palm Desktop are actually different programs. Palm Desktop for Windows was built from scratch, while the Macintosh version is actually a modified version of *Claris Organizer,* a popular contact manager.

Where to Find It

Web Site	Address	What's There
Palm, Inc.	**www.palm.com/macintosh**	Mac-specific Palm information
Chapura	**www.chapura.com**	Outlook synchronization utility PocketMirror
Puma Technologies	**www.pumatech.com**	Contact manager synchronization utility IntelliSync

Chapter 3

Getting Set Up with Your Computer

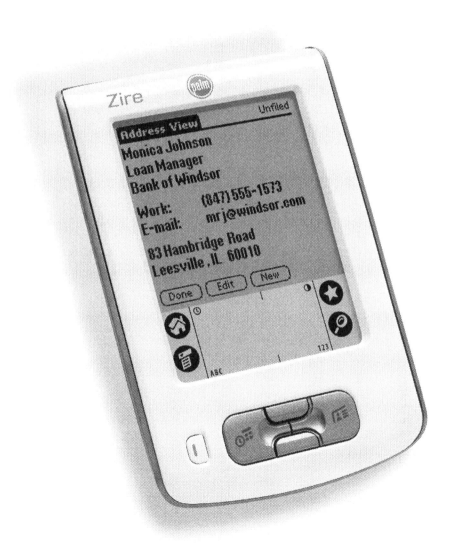

How to...

- Plug in your Zire
- Install the Palm Desktop software
- Set up the HotSync Manager
- Perform your first HotSync
- Interpret the HotSync log
- Keep your data synchronized just the way you like

What makes your spiffy new Zire different than other organizers and gadgets that can store your contacts and schedule? In a nutshell, the Zire connects to your desktop computer via a USB cable, and that lets you keep the stuff on your PC completely in sync with your handheld. There's no need to enter the same name and phone number over again when you first start using your Zire, since it can grab everything off your PC. If you make changes on the Zire or your desktop computer, just reattach the connection cable and sync again later. It's a beautiful system.

To be honest, the Zire wasn't the first handheld device that enabled you to share data with a desktop PC. Dave knows—he's what they call an "early adopter." He still has his old Newton MessagePad, a big PDA sold by Apple that in many ways started the PDA industry in the early 1990s. But synchronizing data on older handheld devices was a chore. Often, the necessary software wasn't included in the box with the handheld itself, and it worked less than optimally. With your Zire, you just tap the Star button and the stuff you use every day is quickly shared. It couldn't be easier.

Since you had the chance to explore your Zire in Chapter 2, it's time to learn about how the device works with your desktop computer. Let's get started!

Plugging It All In

Your Zire comes with a pair of cables. The first, a power adapter, plugs into the upper-left corner of the Zire; let it charge for three to four hours before you start playing with it for the first time. The other cable is a USB HotSync cable. It's used to synchronize information between the Zire and your computer.

You'll probably want to connect the power adapter to a power strip near your PC. That way, you can charge your Zire at your computer desk and perhaps perform a HotSync at the same time. If you plan to synchronize your Zire only occasionally (or never), put the power cable wherever it's most convenient to charge up your PDA every few days.

Connect the USB HotSync cable to a spare USB port on your PC or Macintosh and then plug the other end into the HotSync port on the top of the Zire. Just be sure not to turn on your Zire until after you complete the next step—software installation.

Here are a few things to keep in mind about the HotSync cable:

■ Any USB port will do—you can use an unused port on the front or back of your computer or plug into a USB hub if your computer has one.

■ USB connectors aren't symmetrical, even though they kinda look like they can go in either way. Look carefully at the inside of the flat, rectangular end of the USB cable and you'll see that one side is thicker than the other. If you're having trouble getting it to go into your computer, that's probably why. Flip it over and try again.

■ You don't need to turn off your computer to insert a USB cable, even if people have warned you to shut down your PC before installing equipment. They were talking about other connectors, like serial, parallel, and VGA cables.

 If you're not a computer geek, all this talk about ports may be a bit confusing. What's USB, for instance? USB stands for the Universal Serial Bus and it's a "plug-and-play" port that lets you to connect dozens of devices to your computer quickly and easily.

Installing the Desktop Software

Before you can synchronize your Zire and your desktop PC, you first need to install the Palm Desktop software suite on your computer. Palm Desktop is a personal information manager (PIM). It duplicates all the core applications from your Zire and serves as the headquarters from which you can use synchronized information from your Zire. Though you do need to install Palm Desktop, you don't necessarily need to use it. That is, if you already use Microsoft Outlook, you can synchronize your Zire to that program instead and avoid Palm Desktop entirely.

The CD-ROM that accompanies your Zire includes everything you need to connect the handheld to your desktop, including your choice of synchronization to Palm Desktop or Outlook. Installation is very straightforward. Follow the installation instructions that appear after you insert the CD-ROM.

 Your Zire doesn't have to be synchronized to a desktop computer. If you don't have a PC or if you don't care to sync it, that's fine—but we think you'll enjoy your Zire more if you use the USB cable to keep your appointments, contact information, and other data in sync between the two.

 **About HotSync**

HotSync, a term coined by Palm, Inc., refers to the act of synchronizing the data stored on your handheld and desktop computers. These days, all handheld makers use a special term that means more or less the same thing. Microsoft's Pocket PCs, for instance, use "ActiveSync" instead.

Installing Palm Desktop

The Palm Desktop CD-ROM includes an installer that places some key components on your hard disk. Most of the main installation is completely automated, but you have to make a few decisions:

- **Outlook or Palm Desktop?**   If you have a copy of Microsoft Outlook installed on your PC, the installer detects it and gives you the option of synchronizing your data to it if you so desire (but only if you're a Windows user). What data are we talking about? Stuff like contacts from the address book and appointments from the calendar, as well as notes and tasks. If you're a regular Outlook user and using Windows, you should certainly choose to synchronize your Zire with Outlook. Palm Desktop, on the other hand, is a serviceable PIM, though it's not as comprehensive as Outlook.

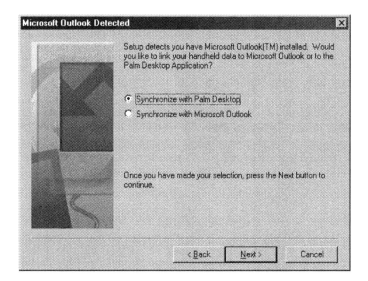

- **Assign a Unique User Name**   The User Name is actually the name of your Zire. You can use your own name or give your PDA a unique descriptor—anything from **Dave's Zire** to **Palm 33A** to just plain **Mike** is acceptable. Is the name important? Yup. If you happen to have more than one Palm-Powered PDA (such as if your spouse has one as well), each one absolutely must have a different name. If you give two or more PDAs the same name, you can end up damaging all the synchronized data on the desktop PC and all the PDAs during a HotSync.

TIP   *If you ever upgrade to a new PDA, you'll probably want to use the same name as your old unit—that way any of your registered software that depends upon the device name will still work on the new PDA. However, if you do that, be sure to reset the old one and give it a different name, since each PDA on your system must have a unique identifier.*

Your First HotSync

Here's what you need to do to make sure you're ready:

- Make sure your HotSync cable is connected to the PC and the Zire.

- Make sure the Zire has a good charge using the power cable. It doesn't need to be plugged in to perform a HotSync.

- Make sure the HotSync Manager software is running on your computer. You should see the HotSync icon in the Windows' System Tray. If you don't see it, start it now. Choose Start | Programs | Palm Desktop | HotSync Manager. If you're on the Mac, it's located in the Chooser or Palm folder.

> **TIP** *The System Tray is the region at the bottom of the Windows Desktop that's found to the right of the Taskbar. It contains the clock and icons for special programs like the HotSync Manager.*

Tapping the HotSync Button

Ready? Turn on your Zire and tap the star-shaped button to the right of the Graffiti area. This is what should happen:

1. You'll hear three tones indicating that the HotSync has begun.

2. A message box appears on the Windows desktop that informs you of the HotSync status.

3. You hear another set of tones when the HotSync is complete.

4. The Zire's screen displays a message indicating that the HotSync is complete.

> **NOTE** *If you already have another Palm OS PDA installed on the PC, the first time you try to HotSync, HotSync Manager will display a dialog box asking you to choose a user name for this new device.*

Exploring the HotSync Manager

The HotSync Manager software does exactly what it sounds like—it manages the connection between your Zire and your computer, enabling you to HotSync. It contains all the options and configurations needed to keep the two devices talking to each other. To HotSync, you needn't mess with anything on the Zire at all. You need to tweak only the HotSync Manager (and that only rarely, if ever).

To get to the HotSync Manager's options in Windows, you need to see the HotSync menu. Click the HotSync Manager icon in the System Tray, and a context menu appears.

> **TIP** *In Windows, you can click the HotSync Manager icon with either the right or left mouse button; the result is the same.*

The Best Films of All Time

Dave: There's no way a rational person could disagree . . . *Aliens* is the best movie of all time. Space Marines fighting xenomorphs with 23rd century machine guns! Woo hoo! What could possibly be cooler than that? And it has some of the best movie lines ever. This, mind you, is the film in which Bill Paxton made the words, "Game over, man," a part of my daily lexicon. After *Aliens,* though, my list gets a bit more introspective. *The Matrix, The Sixth Sense, Almost Famous, Memento,* and *O Brother, Where Art Thou* have to be some of the most amazing films ever made. Now let's see what lame movies Rick thinks are cool. My prediction: His favorite films include *Tron, Dirty Dancing,* and *Weekend at Bernie's 2.*

Rick: I've had just about enough of your *Weekend at Bernie's 2* bashing, mister. Don't make me tell everyone about your strange fondness for Will Smith. Anyway, in no particular order, my Top Five Movies are as follows: *Life is Beautiful, City Lights, The Shawshank Redemption, Toy Story 2,* and *Star Trek II: The Wrath of Khan.* Yes, I know only one of those movies has things blowing up, which means you won't care for the other four. The age of *Ah*-nold has passed, leatherneck. Grow up already.

Three options are the first thing you encounter in the HotSync menu:

- Local USB
- Local Serial
- Modem

 If you're using this on a laptop computer, you'll also see an "infrared" option.

The only one that must be checked is Local USB. This means you can perform a HotSync using the USB port.

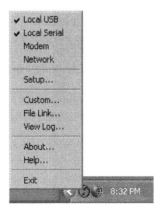

Configuring HotSync Setup

Click the Setup option on the HotSync menu. You should now see the Setup dialog box. This is the place where you get to configure how the HotSync manager behaves. Four tabs are on the Setup dialog box.

General The General tab lets you specify how often the HotSync Manager "listens" to the USB or serial port for a HotSync request. It has three options, as you can see in Figure 3-1:

- **Always available** This is the default setting. As soon as you tap the HotSync button, you synchronize your data. It's fast and convenient, and is probably the way most people use their PDAs.

- **Available only when the Palm Desktop is running** This option isn't all that useful, but it does keep the HotSync manager from running except when the Palm Desktop is running, when you might want to HotSync.

- **Manual** Just like it sounds, the HotSync Manager doesn't run at all unless you choose it from the Start menu (Start | Programs | Palm Desktop | HotSync Manager). This is the least convenient of all the options, but you might want to choose it if you only HotSync on rare occasions.

> **NOTE** *On the Macintosh, these options are slightly different. Start HotSync Manager and choose HotSync | Options. On the HotSync Controls tab, you can enable or disable HotSyncing and specify whether the HotSync Manager should start when you turn on the computer.*

Local The Local tab is where you specify the serial port and speed for your HotSync—but since your Zire uses USB, this tab doesn't apply. It's designed for older PDAs that have serial ports.

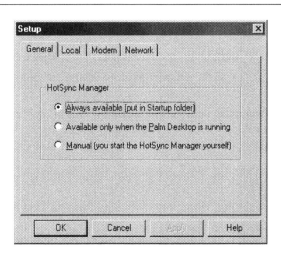

FIGURE 3-1 The General tab determines when the HotSync Manager runs and how easy it is to perform a HotSync.

Modem   This tab is used to specify settings for a more advanced HotSync technique: connecting to your PC via a modem that's attached to your Zire. You don't need to worry about this option, especially since there are no modems for the Zire (at least as of when we wrote this chapter).

After you've seen all the tabs in the Setup dialog box, click OK to save changes or click Cancel to leave the dialog box without changing anything.

Customizing the HotSync Operation

From the HotSync Manager menu, choose Custom.

On the Mac, choose HotSync | Conduit Settings.

This is arguably the most important dialog box in the HotSync software because it lets you to specify exactly what data will get transferred. Before we look at this dialog box, however, we should define a few essential terms the Zire uses to perform data synchronizations. If you make the wrong choice, you can lose data.

Synchronize the files	Suppose you added new files to both the PC and the Zire since the last HotSync. The new data from the Zire is copied to the PC, and the new data from the PC is copied to the Zire. Both devices will have a copy of everything. *This is the best setting to use most of the time and is, in fact, the default for most conduits.*
Desktop overwrites handheld	This option supposes the desktop data is correct at the expense of anything that might be on the handheld. If you add new files to both the PC and the handheld, for instance, and then perform this kind of sync, the new files on the Zire will be lost. The desktop data overwrites whatever was on the Zire.
Handheld overwrites desktop	This is exactly the opposite of the previous case. Assuming the handheld data is more correct for some reason (we assume you have your reasons), any files that are different or new on the desktop PC are lost after the synchronization. Both systems will have the Zire data.
Do nothing	With this option selected, no changes are made to either device.

Remember that each conduit can be adjusted separately. This means you can set the Date Book to overwrite the PC's Address Book, while the e-mail conduit is set to Do Nothing and the Notes conduit synchronizes.

What's a Conduit?

Conduit is the term Palm, Inc., uses to describe the software that connects data on your Zire with similar data on your computer. The Calendar conduit, for instance, makes sure the Zire's Date Book and the computer's calendar (be it in Palm Desktop or Outlook) stay completely in sync. Every application on your Zire that has a corresponding program on the PC is connected with its own conduit, and the Custom menu option is where you turn to adjust these conduits.

If you're ever in doubt about the state of your conduits, be sure to check the action before you press the HotSync button by right-clicking the HotSync icon and choosing Custom.

3

With those terms in mind, let's look at the Custom dialog box. As you can see in Figure 3-2, the top of the box displays the name of the PDA. Managing more than one Palm-Powered device from each PC is possible, so you select the proper unit from the list menu before continuing. If you only have a single Zire, don't worry about this option.

To configure a conduit, either double-click an entry or select it, and then click the Change button. Depending on which conduit you open, you'll find you might have all four synchronization options (as in Figure 3-3) or, perhaps, fewer.

When you configure a conduit, whatever selection you make applies only to the very next time you HotSync unless you check the box for Set As Default.

HotSync as a Way of Life

After your first HotSync, you may begin to see how convenient it is to have a duplicate of your desktop data on your Zire—and vice versa. If the battery in your Zire dies, for instance, just HotSync to restore everything. The only data you may lose is anything you entered in the PDA since the last HotSync.

But how often should you HotSync? The short answer is as frequently as you like. Some people HotSync daily, while others—whose data changes much less frequently—update their Zire only once a week or even less. Use this guide as a rule of thumb:

■ HotSync before you leave the house with your PDA.

■ HotSync when you return from a trip to update your PC with new info stored on the Zire.

■ HotSync to install new programs on your Zire (this is discussed in Chapter 4).

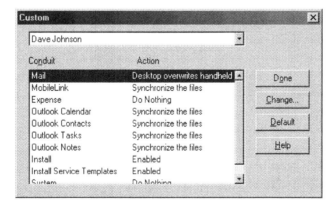

FIGURE 3-2   The Custom dialog box enables you to specify how each conduit behaves when you HotSync.

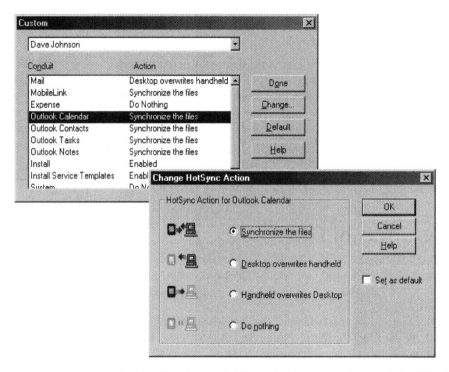

FIGURE 3-3   You can change each conduit whenever you like before a HotSync.

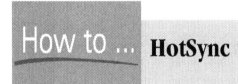 **HotSync**

- Plug the Zire into your PC.
- Make sure the HotSync Manager software is running (by default, it always should be).
- Verify that the conduits are set properly to transfer and synchronize data just the way you want.
- Turn on your Zire.
- Tap the star-shaped HotSync button on the Zire.
- Wait until you hear the HotSync complete tones before disconnecting the Zire from the sync cable.

Changing Conduits On-the-Fly

Often you may find yourself changing all the conduits in your HotSync Manager except one or two. You might want to disable everything except the Install conduit to quickly get a new program onto your Zire, for instance, or set everything except AvantGo to Do Nothing so you can get your news onto the PDA as you're running out the door to lunch.

Whatever the reason, you'll soon find that there's no easy way to disable several conduits at once. Using the HotSync Manager to change five conduits to Do Nothing is almost as time consuming as just doing the whole darned HotSync to begin with.

There's an easier way. Download the tremendously useful program called Ultrasoft NotSync from PalmGear.com. This program lets you quickly and easily change your conduits in just seconds. The change only applies to the very next HotSync, so it never affects your default settings.

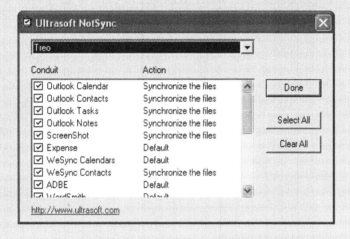

What HotSync Does to Files

After your first HotSync, you have a set of data on both your Zire and your desktop. The goal of the HotSync process is to make sure the data stays the same on both systems. So what happens when you change data on one or both of the computers?

This table, which assumes the conduit is set to synchronize the files, should help you understand the subtleties of the HotSync:

Before the HotSync	After the HotSync
You add a file to the Zire (or the PC).	That file is added to the PC (or the Zire).
You delete a file from the Zire (or PC).	The file is also deleted from the PC (or Zire).
You change a file on the Zire.	The file is changed on the PC.
You changed the same file on both the Zire and PC—they're now different.	Both versions of the file are added to both the Zire and PC. You need to modify the file and delete the one you don't want to keep.

TIP   *Don't forget, you can configure each conduit individually, so the Address Book might be set to Synchronize the files, while the Date Book is set to Desktop Overwrites Handheld, for instance.*

Chapter 4

Getting Information In and Out of Your Zire

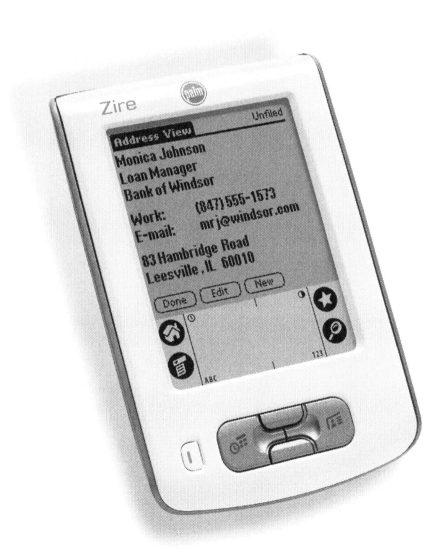

How to...

- Use Graffiti to enter data into your Zire
- Type using the onscreen keyboard
- Enter data using the Palm Desktop
- Display Graffiti help
- Receive data from another PDA via infrared
- Beam items to another PDA
- Beam your business card to another PDA
- Install new software on your Zire
- Delete old applications from your Zire

Your Zire is only as good as the information you store inside it, or, perhaps more to the point, it's only as good as the methods you have for getting information into it. After all, if you make storing your appointments on the computer too difficult, you won't bother doing it—and then you own an expensive paperweight with the word "Zire" written on it.

You already know about some of the tools at your disposal for getting data in and out of your PDA. We talked about how to HotSync in Chapter 3, and you know you can enter data directly in the device using Graffiti, an almost ordinary style of handwriting. In this chapter, you learn everything you might ever need to know about Graffiti. We also cover other data entry methods, including the onscreen keyboard and beaming data directly between PDAs using the built-in IR port.

The Three Ways to Enter Data

Without a doubt, one of the first things you want to do with your new Zire is enter text and numbers into your various applications. Hey, don't look so surprised. The core applications, like Date Book, Address List, Memo Pad, and To Do List, rely on you to fill them with interesting things you can later reference.

Unlike some handheld computers, the Zire doesn't include a keyboard. Instead, you can use any one of three completely different methods for entering information into your Zire:

- Enter text using Graffiti.
- Enter text using the onscreen keyboard.
- Enter text into the Palm Desktop, and then HotSync the data to your Zire.

Using Graffiti

Graffiti is a specialized handwriting recognition system that enables you to enter text almost error-free. Unlike other handwriting recognition systems, Graffiti doesn't interpret your ordinary handwriting. Instead, you need to slightly modify the way you write and make specific kinds of pen strokes that represent the letters, numbers, and punctuation you're trying to write. Don't worry, though, this isn't hard to do. You can learn the basics of Graffiti inside of a day—heck, you can probably master most of the characters in an hour or less.

When entering text into your Zire, you can't write directly on the part of the screen the Zire uses to display data. Instead, you write inside the small rectangle at the bottom of the display—the one that sits between the four icons. We call this the *Graffiti area*.

TIP   *There's a Palm OS utility called TealEcho that lets you write above the Graffiti area, right on the main screen. Some people find this way of entering text more intuitive because the characters appear directly under where they're writing. See Chapter 13 for more information on this tool.*

The rectangle is divided roughly in half: the left side is used to enter letters, while the right side is used to enter numbers.

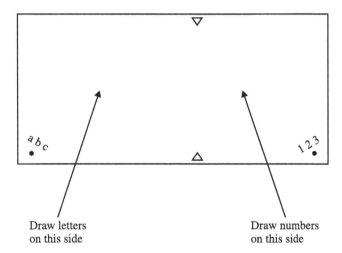

Draw letters
on this side

Draw numbers
on this side

TIP   *If you aren't getting the results you expect from Graffiti, make sure you're writing on the correct side of the rectangle. The right side is for numbers, the left side is for letters, and either side works for punctuation.*

Graffiti characters are letters you make with a single stroke of the stylus (they're called *gestures* in Graffiti-ese). The characters must be drawn in a very specific way: when you see these gestures drawn in print, such as here in this book, the dot indicates the starting position. To write a character, mimic the gesture by drawing the shape starting with the dot and—in most cases—finish the character in a single stroke without lifting the stylus. For more details on writing in Graffiti, see the section "Getting to Know Graffiti," later in this chapter.

Using the Onscreen Keyboard

Even after you get comfortable writing with Graffiti, you'll sometimes want to input characters without using pen strokes. All it takes to use the keyboard is a tap. At the bottom of the Graffiti area, you see the letters *ABC* on the left and the numbers *123* on the right. Tap either spot to call up the appropriate keyboard (alpha or numeric).

 *In applications that require you to enter a password or registration code, tapping it out on the keyboard is easier than writing it with Graffiti. With the keyboard, you can be sure you're entering exactly the right characters.*

Once the keyboard is open, note that you can switch between letters and numbers by tapping the selector at the bottom of the screen. A set of international characters is available as well.

 *The keyboard appears only where it's appropriate—specifically, when a cursor is in a data field. If no application is open into which you can insert text, you'll simply hear a beep when you try to open the keyboard.*

Using Palm Desktop

Those methods are great when you're on the go, but what about getting data into your Zire when you're comfortably sitting at your desk? Nothing is wrong with entering notes with Graffiti, but long notes can get tiresome. Instead, use the keyboard on your desktop PC to type into the Zire much more quickly and efficiently.

How? By using Palm Desktop or another program with a HotSync conduit. Suppose you need to enter a long note into your Zire. Instead of writing it with Graffiti, create a note in Palm Desktop or Outlook (depending on which program you use) and then HotSync.

Let's add a note to the Zire's Memo Pad using Palm Desktop. Do this:

1. Start Palm Desktop.

2. In Windows, switch to the Memo Pad view by clicking the Memo button on the left side of the screen. On the Mac, choose View | Note List.

3. If you're using Windows, start typing. On the Mac, click the Create Note button on the toolbar at the top of the screen.

4. When you finish typing your note, close the New Note dialog box (on the Mac) or click anywhere in the Memo list (in Windows). The note is automatically saved, and the memo's subject line shows as much of the note as would fit on the line in the list.

5. When you finish entering data, HotSync—the data will be transferred to your Zire.

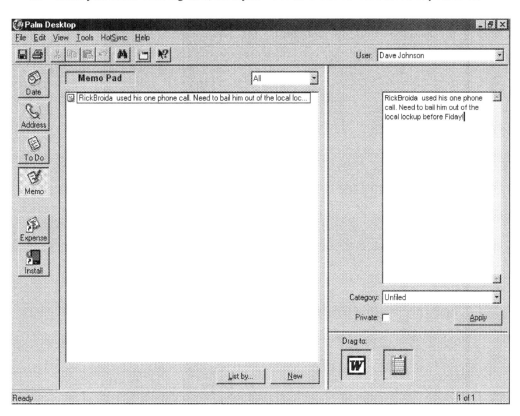

Getting to Know Graffiti

Earlier in the chapter, we took a quick look at using Graffiti to enter data into your Zire. Graffiti is the principal way of interfacing with your favorite PDA, so knowing Graffiti like the back of your hand is essential to using your Zire effectively.

Part of learning to use Graffiti is memorizing the character set. Another part is modifying the way you write. Instead of writing characters one next to the other (as on paper), you write one on top of the other. In other words, you don't move across the Graffiti area, from the left side to the right side. You write a letter or number, lift your stylus, then write the next one in the exact same spot. Once you train yourself to do this, you'll have a much easier time mastering Graffiti.

Graffiti is designed to recognize specific gestures as characters, thus reducing the possibility of error. In fact, you should get just about 100 percent accuracy all the time. Graffiti doesn't have to understand 50 different ways of making the letter *T*, so it's both fast and accurate.

> **TIP** *There's a Graffiti cheat sheet built into the Zire. By default, you can see it by drawing a line from the Graffiti area to the top of the LCD screen.*

General Tips and Tricks for Graffiti

Before we get started with the nuts and bolts of writing with Graffiti, it might help to remember a few things. Despite Graffiti's simplicity, a few tips and tricks can make writing on the Zire a lot easier.

- Draw your characters as large as possible. Use all the Graffiti area, if necessary.
- Don't cross the line between the letter and number portion of the Graffiti area. Make sure you make your gestures on the correct side of the fence.
- Don't write at a slant. Remember the way you learned to draw your letters in first grade? Nice and straight—that's how they should be on the Zire, too.
- Don't write too fast. Graffiti doesn't care about speed, but if you write too fast, you might get sloppy.
- If you have a hard time making certain gestures consistently, try a different way. See Table 4-1 for a list of primary and secondary gestures for each character, and use the ones that work best for you.

Writing Letters and Numbers

Almost every letter and number at your disposal has two important characteristics:

- Every letter and number can be drawn in a single stroke without lifting the stylus off the screen.
- Every letter and number bears a strong resemblance to its normal, plain English counterpart.

Letter	Gestures	Letter	Gestures
A	∧	S	S 5
B	B B 3	T	7 ⟩
C	C <	U	U ✓
D	D D △	V	V V
E	E ξ	W	W W
F	Γ Γ	X	X ⤫
G	G G	Y	y γ
H	h h	Z	Z 2
I	I	0	O O U
J	J J	1	I ∧
K	∝	2	2 Z
L	L ∠	3	3
M	m m	4	L <
N	N ∞	5	5 5
O	O O	6	6 ∂
P	P P	7	7 ⊃ ⟩
Q	℧ ℧	8	8 8 γ
R	R R	9	9 ξ

TABLE 4-1   The Graffiti Numbers and Letters

4

The easiest way to learn Graffiti is simply to practice writing the alphabet a few times. Use the Graffiti reference sticker that came with your Zire, or refer to Table 4-1 for a guide on how to draw each character. The advantage of using this book, of course, is that we show you a few alternative gestures that might make certain characters easier to draw consistently.

One exception: When you make an *X,* you can pick the stylus up off the screen to cross the letter in the traditional way. Of course, there's also a single-stroke alternative you can use, as well (see Table 4-1 for the scoop on that).

The Hardest Characters

Everyone seems to have trouble with some Graffiti character. Even if you can never get your Zire to recognize your letter *B*, that doesn't make you a freak—it just means you should learn an alternative stroke for that letter or put extra care into drawing it carefully and slowly. Even we have trouble with some letters . . .

Dave: It's unfortunate my last name is "Johnson," because I can't get Graffiti to take my letter *J* to save my life. Half the time, it's my own fault. As many times as I've made the *J*, I can't remember it starts at the top and curves down. I always try to start at the bottom and hook up—which gives me a letter *U* every time. But, even when I remember how to do it, I end up with a *V* or a new paragraph. Of course, now that I'm drawing it for this chapter, I can't seem to do it wrong—ten perfect *J*'s out of ten. I think the letter just hates me. And I know I'm not crazy, by the way, despite what my dog keeps telling me.

Rick: If you'd ever seen Dave's chicken-scratch excuse for handwriting, you'd understand why he sometimes has trouble with Graffiti. To be fair, though, a few characters seem tougher to make than others. It's the *V* that drives me up the wall—I always forget to put the little tail on the end of the upstroke. But I know a secret: if you write the letter backward, it comes out perfectly every time—and you don't need to draw the tail!

You might notice some letters and numbers have identical gestures. The letter *L* and the number 4, for instance, are both made in the same way (see Figure 4-1). How does Graffiti tell the difference? That's an easy one—the Graffiti area is divided into a number side and a letter side.

 *If you're really having trouble mastering Graffiti, there's a great tutorial program called PenJammer (www.penjammer.com). It's not for Windows or Macintosh—it works right on your handheld, teaching you every Graffiti character via animated helpers. Very cool, very helpful, and very inexpensive (it's just $7.95).*

Gesture	Character	
L	L	4
I	I	1
3	B	3

FIGURE 4-1 The letter *L* and the number 4 are made exactly the same. So is the letter *I* and the number 1.

Capitalizing Letters

You've probably noticed that there's no distinction between lowercase and uppercase characters. That's a good thing—you don't have to learn over 100 gestures because uppercase and lowercase letters are drawn the same way. Here's how to tell Graffiti you want to make an uppercase letter:

■ **One capital letter**   To make the next character, draw an uppercase gesture; draw a vertical line from the bottom of the Graffiti area to the top. This only works on the left side of the screen; it won't work in the number area. You see a symbol like this one, which indicates you're now in Uppercase mode:

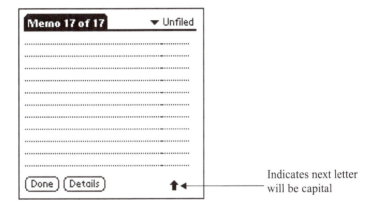

Indicates next letter will be capital

■ **All capital letters**   To switch to All Caps mode and type in all capital letters, draw the vertical gesture twice. You see this symbol to indicate All Caps mode:

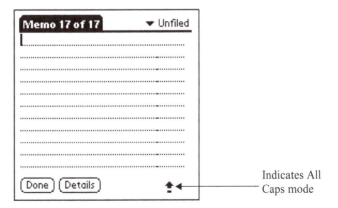

Indicates All Caps mode

■ **Lowercase letters** If you're already in All Caps mode, you can exit and write in lowercase again by making one more vertical gesture. The All Caps symbol should disappear to show that you changed modes.

TIP
One of our all-time favorite Zire programs is called MiddleCaps (see Chapter 13). It saves you having to write the upstroke before each capital letter. Just write the letter across the imaginary line separating the letter and number sides of the Graffiti area. Absolutely indispensable, and it's a freebie! Find it at PalmGear (www.palmgear.com). Make sure to read Chapter 13, too, because you need another program (X-Master) to get MiddleCaps to work.

Spaces, Backspaces, and Deleting Text

Words are arguably more useful when you can put a space between them, thus enabling the reader to discern where each one ends and the next one begins. In Graffiti, it's easy to insert spaces. So easy, in fact, you might be able to figure it out on your own (but we'll tell you anyway). Draw a dash that starts on the left and goes to the right, and the cursor skips ahead a space. You can use this gesture to insert spaces between words or to perform any other space-making task you might need. And, yes, you can insert multiple spaces simply by performing this gesture as many times as needed.

The backspace, not surprisingly, is exactly the opposite. Draw a gesture from right to left and the cursor backs up, deleting any text it encounters along the way.

Using the backspace gesture is great if you want to delete one or two characters, but what if you want to delete a whole sentence? That backspace swipe can get tiring if you have a lot of text to kill or replace all at once. Fortunately, there's an easy solution: select the text you want to delete. The next thing you write replaces the selected text. Here's how to do it:

1. Tap and hold the stylus down at the start of the text you want to select, and then drag the stylus across the text and pick it up when you've selected all the text in question.

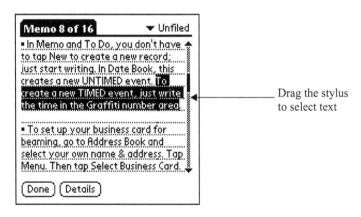

Drag the stylus to select text

2. In the Graffiti area, write some new text. The old text is immediately erased and replaced with the new text. If you simply want to delete the text, use the backspace gesture instead.

Adding Punctuation

To add punctuation to your prose, you need to (surprise, surprise) enter Graffiti's special Punctuation mode. All it takes is a tap in the Graffiti area. You see a dot appear, which indicates that you can now enter punctuation. Table 4-2 displays the punctuation gestures you commonly need.

The most common punctuation mark is a period, and because it's simply a dot, you can add a period to the end of a sentence by performing a quick double-tap. Some other symbols are trickier, though, and may take some practice. The comma, parenthesis bracket, and apostrophe are so similar, for instance, that getting one when you're trying to gesture another isn't unusual.

If you enter the Punctuation mode by tapping on one side of the Graffiti area, you need to complete the punctuation gesture on the same side. Tapping once on the number side and again on the letter side has no effect, for instance.

Getting Help with Graffiti

Graffiti help is never far away. You should know about a few resources that can help you master this almost, but not quite, normal alphabet:

■ **Play a game**   When you start out with Graffiti, you might want to learn with a game. Called Giraffe, it enables you to get up to speed quickly on the art of shaping Graffiti characters. You need to draw the correct gesture for letters that fall from the sky. Time is limited, so a few rounds of Giraffe can builds up your speed and accuracy at drawing letters and numbers.

■ **Display the help screen**   There's a Graffiti reference built into the Zire. To display it, start your stylus at the very bottom of the Graffiti area and draw a vertical line that extends all the way up to the top of the screen.

■ **Use the guides**   Keep the sticker that came with your Zire handy. The tables (Table 4-1 and 4-2) in this chapter are also handy for learning the ropes, though we know you're not likely to carry our book around with you everywhere you go (though we hear that's what all the cool kids are doing).

Beaming Data Between PDAs

On *Star Trek,* transporters are used to beam people and equipment from one location to another. While we're a long way from being able to beam physical things around, your Zire makes it possible to beam almost any kind of data between PDA users. Almost all modern handhelds have

Punctuation	Gestures
Period	•
Comma	╱ (draw low)
Question mark	? ⌐
Exclamation point	╎
Colon	V
Semicolon	⩘
Open parenthesis	C
Close parenthesis	⌐
Tab	⌐
Apostrophe	╎ (draw high)
Quotes	N
Slash	╱
Backslash	╲
At symbol	◯
Asterisk	⅋
Number sign	⋃ ⌐
Greater than	<
Less than	>
Percent	⋃⋃ ⋙
Equal sign	Z
Plus sign	⍺
Dollar sign	S

TABLE 4-2   The Most Common Graffiti Punctuation Gestures

an infrared port, usually at the top of the case. Using this IR port, you can beam information in a surprising number of ways. Here are just some of the things you can do:

- Beam contacts, appointments, or memos to other Palm Powered PDA users.
- Give another PDA user your "business card."
- Print on an IR-equipped printer.
- Play two-player games "head-to-head."
- Send data between your Zire and a cell phone or pager.

4

How to Beam

No matter what you're planning to beam—or receive—the process is essentially the same. Actually seeing the process demonstrated is faster than reading about it; but because neither Dave nor Rick can stop by your house this afternoon, here's the process in a nutshell:

1. Orient the two PDAs so their IR ports face each other, and are between about four inches and three feet apart.
2. The sender chooses the item to beam.
3. The sender chooses the Beam command from the menu.
4. A dialog box appears to indicate the beam is in progress. First, you see a message that your PDA is searching for the other device. That message then goes away, and the data is transmitted.

5. After the beam, the sending Zire goes back to business as usual—you won't get a message indicating the beam was successful. The receiver, on the other hand, gets a dialog box that asks permission to accept the beamed data.

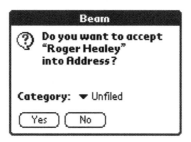

Selecting Items for Beaming

So, now that you know the rudiments of beaming, you're no doubt eager to start. While we're usually a pretty down-to-earth couple of guys, we have to admit a certain coolness factor is involved in beaming things to each other. It's definitely better than writing notes by hand or trading easily scrunched business cards.

Beaming Appointments

If you work with other PDA users, you can make sure everyone is on the same schedule by beaming entries from the date book. To do that, select an appointment and choose Beam Event from the menu.

Beaming Contacts

If you're like most people, the Address List is the most used part of your Zire. Instead of exchanging paper-based business cards, now you can beam the information between Palm OS devices, which can later be HotSynced back to your PC's contact manager. In recognition of just how important the Address List is, you have not one, not two, but three options for sending data from this application:

- ■ **Beam the current entry**   To send an Address List entry to another user, find the name you want in the Address List and choose Beam Address from the menu.

- ■ **Beam a whole bunch of entries**   You can send any number of contacts to someone else all at once—every name in your Zire, in fact—using Beam Category. Choose the category you want to beam by picking the category from the list at the upper-right corner of the screen. Then choose Beam Category from the menu.

4

CAUTION   *Be careful before you beam or try to receive a whole category's worth of contacts— make sure it's something you really need to do. This operation could include hundreds of entries, which will take more time than either of you are willing to spend pointing your PDAs at each other.*

- ■ **Beam your own entry**   What's more common than handing your business card to someone? You can configure your own Address List entry as your personal business card and beam it to other PDAs. For details on configuring an entry as your business card, see Chapter 6. Once configured, however, you can send it by holding down the Address List button for two seconds.

Beaming Memos and Tasks

Memos are handy to pass off to other Palm OS users. You can give them notes, action items, short documents, and even meeting minutes in this way. Likewise, if you want to delegate a task to someone else in your office, tell that person to "visit my cubicle—and don't forget to bring your Zire." There are two ways to beam memos and to-do items:

- **Beam a Memo or a To Do** To beam a single item, select it and choose Beam Memo (for a Memo) or Beam Item (for a To Do) from the menu.

- **Beam a bunch of stuff at once** Like the Address List, you can select a category in the Memo List or the To Do List and then choose Beam Category from the menu. To beam all your memos or tasks at once, remember to set the category list to All.

Beaming Applications

Now for the best part: You can transfer entire programs from one Palm Powered PDA to another. If you meet someone who shows you a cool new game or utility, for instance, you can ask for a copy right away.

Not all programs can be beamed. The core apps that come with your Zire are "locked," making them nonbeamable. Many commercial programs are also locked. In addition, if you have a program that requires supporting files, it won't be beamable. This means you must go home and install the program the old-fashioned way, using your PC.

Now that we've told you what you can't do, let's talk about what you can do. Beaming an application isn't much different than beaming data from one of the Zire's programs. Do this:

1. Tap the Home button on your Zire to return to applications.

2. From the menu, choose Beam. You see a dialog box with a list of all the applications on your Zire, as in Figure 4-2. Some applications have little locks; these aren't beamable.

3. Select an application and tap the Beam button.

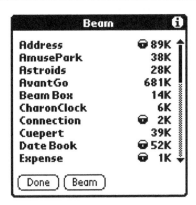

FIGURE 4-2   Choose an app from the list to beam it to another PDA.

Installing New Software on Your Zire

Thousands of free and inexpensive applications are out there, just waiting to be installed. They include enhancements to the core applications, utilities, games, and more. You've only got about 1.7MB of free memory on your Zire, so you can't fit 'em all. But most Palm OS applications are pretty small, so there's room for a bunch. You might wonder: how the heck do I get all this cool stuff onto my Zire?

The answer is that the Palm Desktop includes a handy Install tool for loading apps.

4

Prepping Applications for Installation

Often, downloaded applications aren't immediately ready for installation. If you download an application from the Internet, it usually arrives in the form of a SIT file (if you're a Mac user) or a ZIP file (if you use Windows). You need to expand these files before they can be installed on your Zire. We recommend these tools for managing compressed files:

- ■ **Windows**   Use WinZip to uncompress ZIP files.
- ■ **Macintosh**   Use Aladdin StuffIt Expander to manage SIT files.

Of course, if you already happily expand compressed files with another program, keep up the good work; these are just our favorites.

Once expanded, most Palm OS files bear the file extension .PRC or .PDB. In a ZIP or SIT with lots of little files, you generally just grab the PRC and PDB files and install those. Of course, if in doubt, read whatever documentation accompanied the application. It usually tells you exactly what files need to be installed.

Removing Applications from the Zire

You won't want every application you install on your PDA forever. Some programs you won't like, others will outlive their usefulness; and, quite often, you need to eliminate some apps to make room for more because the Zire has limited storage space.

Deleting programs is easy. Tap the Home icon on your Zire; then tap Menu | App | Delete. You see a list of all the applications currently stored on the handheld. At the top of the screen, you also see a bar that shows how much memory remains on your Zire.

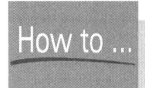

How to ... Install New Applications

1. Start the Palm Desktop by choosing Start | Programs | Palm Desktop | Palm Desktop. On the Mac, select the Palm Desktop from the Chooser or the Palm folder.

2. Click the Install button on the left side of the Palm Desktop screen. The Install tool appears. If you're using a Mac, choose HotSync | Install from the menu.

3. Click the Add button. You see the Open dialog box for selecting applications.

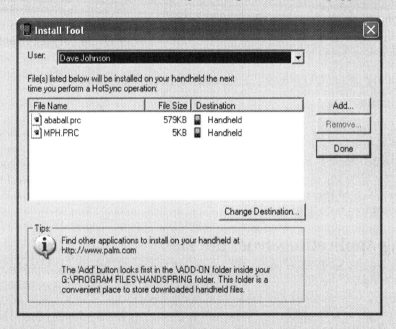

4. Locate the program you want to install and select it. Click the Open button.

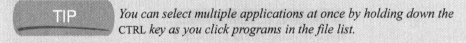 *You can select multiple applications at once by holding down the* CTRL *key as you click programs in the file list.*

5. With your application displayed in the Install Tool dialog box, click Done.

6. The next time you HotSync your Zire, the selected application is installed.

To delete an application, select it and tap the Delete button. This is similar to the Beam interface, and, in fact, it's so similar that you should be careful you don't accidentally delete an app you're trying to beam to a friend.

Chapter 5 The Date Book

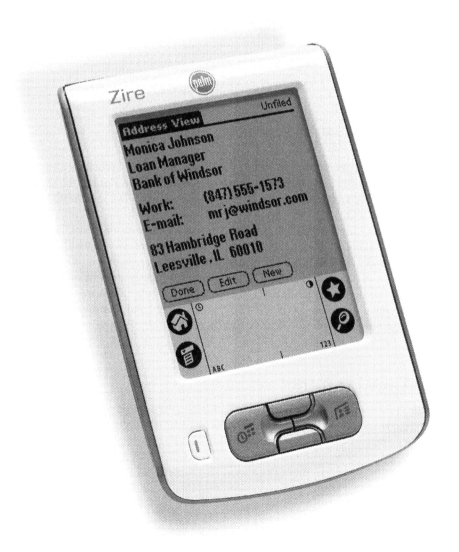

How to...

- Use the Day, Week, Month, and Agenda Views
- Customize the Date Book's appearance
- Add appointments to the Date Book
- Beam an appointment to someone else
- Create an appointment using the Address Book
- Create repeating appointments
- Add a note
- Make an appointment private
- Edit appointments
- Delete events
- Set an alarm
- Use the Zire with your desktop computer

Are you busy on Tuesday at 3 P.M.? If you had your Zire handy, you'd probably already know the answer to that question. In an informal survey, we found the Date Book is the single most popular core application on the Zire. Truly, some people buy their PDA just for its scheduling prowess.

The Date Book is a modern miracle. That may sound like an overstatement, but consider how useful it is. It can track all your appointments. It can show you your schedule by day, week, or month. The Date Book handles recurring appointments and can alarm you about upcoming events. It synchronizes precisely with your desktop calendar, like Palm Desktop or Microsoft Outlook, and the Date Book fits in the palm of your hand. It's better, Rick might tell you, than Britney Spears and Culture Club combined. Dave, on the other hand, has some culture and would be inclined to say it's better than The Beatles. On the other hand, no, there's nothing better than The Beatles.

View Your Appointments

Start the Date Book by pressing the Date Book button on your Zire (it's the one on the left) or tapping the Date Book icon in the Zire's Application screen. When you launch Date Book, by default it shows a calendar listing for the current day.

Navigate the Day View

When you start the Date Book, the first thing you see is the Day View. You can see that it shows the currently selected date in the tab at the top of the screen. Next to that are seven letters, one for each day of the week.

Last week

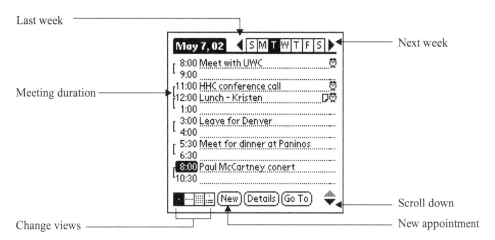

Meeting duration

Next week

Scroll down

Change views

New appointment

5

Tap and hold the Date tab to see the current time. If you let go too quickly, the menu will drop instead.

In the middle of the screen, you see the current day's calendar. You can enter new events on the blank lines. If you have any appointments already entered, note that appointments lasting for more than 30 minutes have duration brackets. *Duration brackets* appear to the immediate left of the appointment time and show you what time an appointment is scheduled to end.

Other icons also appear near appointments. In fact, you should get used to seeing these three icons:

- **Alarms**   This icon indicates you'll be notified by the alarm sound that the appointment is due to start.

- **Notes**   If you attach a note to your appointment (perhaps with directions to the location or agenda details, for instance) you see this icon.

- **Repeating meetings**   If the meeting is configured to happen more than once, this icon appears.

If you tap any of these icons, seen in Figure 5-1, you see the Event Details dialog box, which we discuss in detail later in this chapter.

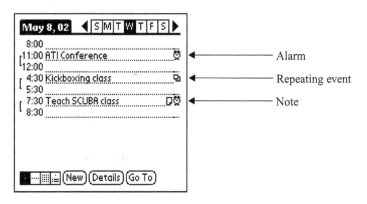

FIGURE 5-1   These icons tell you valuable information about your appointment. Tap them to edit the details.

Finally, the bottom of the screen has several important controls. Icons exist to change the current View, as well as to create a new appointment, to View the Event Details dialog box, and to go to a specific day.

Change View Options

By default, the Day View compresses your calendar by not showing blank times of the day. This way, you can have appointments that span from 6 A.M. to 11 P.M. and have them all appear onscreen without needing to scroll at all. Whenever it can, it includes blank events between existing events for better readability.

What happens if you have such a busy day that all your appointments won't fit onscreen at once, even with the Zire's compression in place? You need to tap the Scroll button at the bottom of the screen. It only appears when needed.

NOTE   *Lots of users try using the Scroll button on the Zire's case to see more appointments in the same day. Instead, pressing the Scroll button actually changes the View to the next day.*

Not everyone likes the Day View compression. If you frequently add events to your schedule during the day, for instance, you might want to have blank lines available for all the hours of the day. If this sounds like you, here's how to turn off compression:

1. Choose Options | Display Options from the menu.

2. Uncheck the Compress Day View option.

3. Tap the OK button.

Now when you use the Day View, you see all the blank lines for your day. On the other hand, using this setting virtually guarantees you need to use the stylus to surf around your daily schedule.

When you configure your Day View, you also have to decide what kind of person you are. Are you

- Neat and orderly—and opt for less clutter whenever possible?

- Impatient—and want everything at your fingertips all the time?

- Apathetic—and don't want to bother changing the default settings?

You can change the display of the Date Book to accommodate the way you want your Zire to look. If you're the neat and orderly sort, for instance, you might want the Date Book to be a blank screen, unless it actually has appointments already scheduled for that day. If this is the case, choose Options | Preferences and set the Start Time and End Time to be the same thing—like 7:00 A.M. After configuring your Zire in this way, you should find that days without appointments are essentially a blank screen with a single blank line—the time you set in Preferences.

More the impatient sort? Then choose Options | Preferences and configure your Start Time and End Time to span the full range of hours you plan to use. If you ever add events to the evening, for instance, set the End Time for 10 P.M. or later. This way, you have a blank line available immediately for writing a new entry.

If all this sounds extremely pointless to you, leave the Preferences alone. The default settings cover most of the hours you routinely need.

Getting Around the Days of the Week

There are several ways to change the View to a different day. You can figure out most of them on your own, but we bet you can't find 'em all. Here's how to do it—use the method that's easiest for you.

- Switch to a specific day by tapping the appropriate day icon at the top of the screen.

- To move ahead one week at a time, use the forward button to the right of the week icons. If you're currently on Tuesday, for instance, tapping the arrow takes you one week ahead to the following Tuesday. Obviously, you can go back a week at a time by tapping the Back arrow instead.

- To move forward or backward one day at a time, press the Scroll button. If you hold it down, you scroll quickly, like holding down a repeating key on a computer keyboard.

- If you want to find a specific day quickly, tap the Go To button and enter the date directly in the Go to Date dialog box. When you use Go To, remember to choose the year and month first because you go to the selected date as soon as you tap a date.

- To get back to "today" from somewhere else in the calendar, tap Go To and then tap Today on the Go to Date calendar dialog box.

Navigate the Week View

Now that you're used to the Day View, we'll let you in on a little secret: there's more where that came from. That's where the icons at the bottom of the screen come in. Tap the second one to change to the Week View.

TIP
The Date Book button also serves as a View changer. Every time you press the button, the View cycles from Day View to Week View to Month View to Agenda View and back to Day View again. It's convenient to jab with your thumb as you view your various schedule screens.

This screen uses a grid to display your appointments. The top of the grid is labeled by day and date, while the left side contains time blocks throughout the day. The gray blocks represent scheduled events. Obviously, this view isn't ideal for determining your daily schedule in detail, but it's handy for getting your week's availability at a glance. Use it to pick a free day or to clear an afternoon, for instance, when you're in a meeting and trying to choose a good time to get together with an equally busy person.

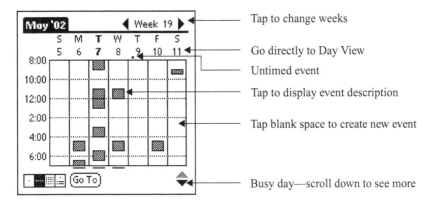

Tap to change weeks
Go directly to Day View
Untimed event
Tap to display event description
Tap blank space to create new event
Busy day—scroll down to see more

If you have an appointment you need to move to another time anywhere in the week, tap the event, hold the stylus down and drag it to another place on the schedule. As you move the block around, you can see the exact time to which the event is being moved. To abort this process without changing anything, move it back to its original location without lifting the stylus.

Navigate the Month View

If you press the Date Book button again or tap the third icon at the bottom of the screen, you're transported to the Month View. It displays an entire month at a time.

Blocks of busy time are now replaced by little hash marks. You can't tap on these marks to see the appointment details because they don't actually represent individual events. Instead, the three possible marks represent events in the morning, afternoon, and evening, as seen in Figure 5-2. In addition, this view shows untimed events as plus signs and multiday events as a series of dots that span several days. If you tap any day in this View, you're automatically taken to the Day View for that day.

By default, both of these special display features are disabled on your Zire. To turn them on, choose Options | Display Options from the Day View screen. Then, in the Month View section of the Display Options dialog box, enable Show Untimed Events and Show Daily Repeating Events.

Manage Your Day from the Agenda View

The last of the Date Book views—the Agenda View—is a favorite for many people. Why is the Agenda View so great? Because it combines your appointments and To Do tasks into a single screen. You can see at a single glance all your responsibilities for the day without switching screens or pressing buttons.

Morning events

Evening events

Untimed event

Multiday event

FIGURE 5-2 If you enable the right features in preferences, you can see untimed and multiday events in the monthly calendar.

Take a look at the Agenda View:

You can see that the top of the screen shows you any appointments and untimed events that may be scheduled for the day. After a horizontal line, your Zire lists your To Dos.

You can change the current day by tapping the arrows at the top of the screen to change a day at a time. If you want to hop directly to another day, tap the date between the arrows. This displays the Go To Date dialog box, just as if you had tapped the Go To button at the bottom of the screen.

To jump to the current date, tap the Go To button and then tap the Today button at the bottom of the Go To Date dialog box.

The Best Sci-Fi

Dave: The Zire is like science fiction come alive, which begs the question, which sci-fi? Rick obsesses over some of the lamest sci-fi shows ever, like *Star Trek: Deep Space Nine* and *The West Wing* (Martin Sheen as the president? Yeah, that's gotta be sci-fi). I am partial to shows with plausible technology, engaging plots, and a real sense of drama—that's why *Babylon 5* ranks up there among the best television ever. Meanwhile, Rick is watching a repeat of another "very special" episode about Kira. Apparently, she lost the bracelet her mom gave her this week.

Rick: Speaking of sci-fi, aliens have taken over Dave's brain. I know because for years… years…I have stated my disdain for *Deep Space Nine* and my total love for *Star Trek: Voyager.* But alien-Dave can't seem to compute that. And, obviously, anyone who doesn't like *The West Wing* must be controlled by some evil influence. Oh, that's right, Dave's a Republican.

The Agenda Zoom

The Agenda View is great for viewing your day's schedule, but it's also a cool way to make changes to your daily itinerary. Just tap on a calendar item to switch to the Day View so you can make schedule changes. Or tap a To Do item to go to the To Do list for editing.

It would be great if you could automatically start your Zire in Agenda View all the time. Alas, you can't quite do that. If you're in a hurry, remember, you can always press the Date Book button several times to cycle through the Date Book's various screens to arrive at the Agenda View.

Create New Appointments

Now that you've mastered the fine art of viewing your schedule from every conceivable angle and perspective, you probably want to know how to add new events to the schedule. As you can probably guess, two ways exist to add appointments to your Zire: via the Palm Desktop—which we discuss later in this chapter—and right from the Zire itself. The only place you can actually enter data about a meeting is from the Day View.

Add Timed Events

Most of the time, your schedule will be full of meetings that take place at a specific time of day, such as

```
Meet with Susan from accounting
3-5 pm in Conference Room A.
```

This is what the Zire refers to as a *timed event*—but most people call it an appointment. In any event, there are three ways to add an event like this to your Zire:

- **Use the New button** Tap the New button on the Day View. Then, within the Set Time dialog box, select a Start Time and an End Time and tap OK. Now, enter the meeting information on the blank line provided for you.

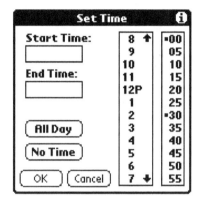

- **Start writing** Tap on a blank line that corresponds to the meeting start time and write the details of the meeting on the line.

- **Pick a time from the Week View** If you're looking for a free space to place a meeting, the Week View is a good place to look because it gives you the "big picture" of your schedule. When you find a spot you like, tap it, and the Day View should open to the desired start time. Then write the meeting info.

 *A fast way to create a new event at a specific time is to write the start time in the Graffiti area. A Set Time dialog box appears, and you can proceed from there. For example, writing a 4 automatically launches the Set Time dialog box for 4 P.M.*

Add Untimed Events

If we wrote about something called a timed event, you must have assumed we'd get to something called an untimed event, right? *Untimed events* are pretty much what you'd expect—they're events associated with a day, but not with a specific time. Typical untimed events include birthdays and anniversaries, reminders to pick up the dry cleaning, and deadline reminders (though you might also consider putting those kinds of things in the To Do list, described in Chapter 7). To create an untimed event, perform one of these two techniques:

- On the Day View with no time selected (in other words, the cursor isn't waiting in a blank line for you already), just start writing. The event appears at the top of the screen as an untimed event.

5

■ Tap New to display the Set Time dialog box. Instead of setting a Start Time and an End Time, though, tap the No Time button and tap OK.

Make Your Appointments Repeat

Some schedule events just don't go away. Weekly meetings, semiannual employee reviews, and the monthly dog grooming sessions are all examples of events you might want the Zire to automate. After all, you don't have the time or energy to write the same weekly event into your Zire 52 times to get it entered for a whole year. An easier way exists. To create a recurring event, do this:

1. Select the entry you want to turn into a recurring event and tap the Details button at the bottom of the Day View screen.

2. In the Event Details dialog box, the Repeat box is currently be set to None—tap it. The Change Repeat dialog box should now appear.

3. Now you need to tap a repeat interval. Will the event repeat daily, weekly, monthly, or annually? In other words, if the event takes place only once a year—or once every five years, tap Year. If you have a meeting that takes place once a month, or every other month, tap Month. For meetings that occur every week or every five weeks, use the Week button. Finally, if you need to schedule daily, every other day, or every-ten-day meetings, tap Day.

4. You now have more options, depending on which interval you choose. A common interval is Week, which would enable you to set up a weekly meeting. Tell the Change Repeat dialog box how often the meeting will occur, such as Every 1 Week or Every 3 Weeks.

5. If you chose a monthly interval, you can also choose whether the meeting will repeat by day (such as the first Monday of every month) or by date (as in the 11th of every month).

6. If the event will repeat more or less forever (or at least as long as you can imagine going to work every day), then leave the End On setting at the default, which is No End Date. If you are creating an event with a clear conclusion, tap End On to set the End Date for this repeating event.

7. Your selection is turned into a plain English description. If you agree the repeat settings are what you want, tap OK.

How to ... Make a Date

If you're setting up an appointment with someone in particular, you can have a lot of fun with your Zire. Okay, it's not better than listening to Pink Floyd with the lights out, but it's pretty cool, nonetheless. Suppose you need to meet with someone who's already in your address book. Switch to the Day View and tap on a blank line at the time you want to start your meeting. Then choose Options | Phone Lookup. You see the Phone Number Lookup dialog box, which displays all the names in your address book. Find the name of the person you're meeting with and tap it. Tap Add. What do you get? The person's name and phone number positioned at the start time of the meeting.

 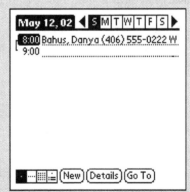

Now it gets even better. Does your friend have a Zire or another Palm Powered PDA? If so, make sure the appointment is still selected and choose Record | Beam Event. You've just given your associate a copy of your meeting in her PDA. She now has no excuse if she is late.

 *If you're attending a multiday event, such as a trade show, you can display this in your Zire by creating an untimed event and setting it to repeat daily (Every 1 Day). Don't forget to set an End Date.*

Make an Appointment Private

You may not want all your appointments to be available to the public. While we generally believe honesty is the best policy, you can flag certain appointments as private—and they'll be hidden from everyone except you. If you want to hide an appointment, do this:

1. On the Day View screen, select an appointment.
2. Tap the Details button.
3. On the Event Details dialog box, tap the Private box to add a check mark. Once you select this option, the current record is flagged for privacy.
4. Tap OK to close the dialog box.

Finally, you'll see an informational dialog box that explains you may yet need to enable the Private Records feature in the Security app. For details on how to do this, see Chapter 9. Using this feature, you can hide and show private data whenever you want.

Edit Recurring Meetings

With most appointments or events, you can make a change just by tapping and entering the needed change with a little Graffiti. Changes to repeating meetings require a little more care. In general, when you change some aspect of a meeting that repeats, the Zire asks you whether you want to change only this one meeting, future meetings, or every meeting in the series.

If you need to move a specific meeting—like the one in November—to a different time, but all the other meetings continue to be held at the traditional time, select Current. The event is actually unlinked from the series and any changes you subsequently make to the rest of the repeating event don't affect the one you changed. On the other hand, if the meeting is moving to a new day permanently, choose All:

There's an exception to this rule: if you change the name of the appointment, then the Zire makes the change to the entire series without asking. If you want to change the text of one instance of the event without changing the rest, you need to unlink it from the series. To do that, try this:

1. Change something else about the event, like its time.

2. You're asked if you want to change the current event or all of the events. Choose Current. The event is now unlinked from the series.

3. Change the name of the unlinked event.

4. If you need to, fix whatever you changed in step 2.

Delete Old Appointments

As time goes on, your Zire starts to accumulate a considerable number of appointments. Often, after an event has passed, you no longer need a record of it. If that's the case, you might want to delete it to save memory. Granted, each appointment takes up a miniscule amount of memory; but eventually this can add up. Even if you don't care about memory savings, meetings do sometimes get canceled—and you need a way to delete them. A few ways exist to get these events off your Zire:

■ **Erase it** Open the Day View. Highlight the text by dragging the stylus over the name of the meeting, and then use a single backspace gesture to erase it.

 *Watch out! If you use this method to delete a repeating event, the Zire erases all the events in the series without warning.*

■ **Use the Delete button** Select the event and tap the Details button. Then tap Delete (or select the item and choose Delete from the menu).

■ **Purge a bunch at once** If you want to delete a bunch of appointments at once, a special tool was designed just for this task. Choose Record | Purge from the Day View. Then choose how much data to delete—you can choose to delete events that are more than a week old or, if you want more of a safety cushion, delete events more than a month old.

 *If you purge your appointments, you have the option to "save an archive copy on PC." If you do that, you can always restore those appointments from the desktop later. To do that, open the Palm Desktop and switch to the Date Book, then choose File | Open Archive from the menu.*

Work with Alarms

If you need a reminder about upcoming events, then you should use the Zire's built-in alarm feature. Any event you enter can be set to beep shortly before the event, giving you enough time to jump in your car, pick up the phone, or start saving for the big day. You can assign an alarm setting to your events as you create the event or at any time afterward.

Pick Your Own Alarm Sound

If, like us, you're easily bored, you might be interested in changing your Zire's default alarm sound. It's easy to do—just visit PalmGear.com and search for alarm sounds. You'll find tons of downloads that give your Zire alternative sounds. Here are a few of the most popular:

- Creationzone Alarm Collection
- System Sound Plus
- GeeSounds

We've listed just three, but the choices are almost limitless. Some apps give you special effects like science fiction or animal sounds, while others are complete songs. If you've ever wanted your Zire to sound like a Star Trek communicator, here's your chance.

Of course, it's not all fun and games—a distinctive alarm sound can make your Zire easier to hear in a crowd.

Timed events play an audible sound. Untimed events don't play a sound, but simply display a screen advising you that the event is pending.

Set Alarms for Specific Events

To enable the alarm for a particular appointment, do this:

1. In the Day View, select an appointment.
2. Tap Details.
3. In the Event Details dialog box, tap the Alarm check box. You should see a new control appear that enables you to set the advance warning for the event.
4. Select how much advanced warning you want. You can choose no warning (enter a zero) or set a time up to 99 days ahead of time. The default is five minutes.

5. Tap OK.

Set Alarms for Everything

By default, the Zire doesn't turn the alarm on for your appointments. Instead, you need to turn the alarm on for every event individually. If you find you like using the alarm, though, you can tell the Zire to turn the alarm on automatically for all your appointments. Then, it's up to you to turn the alarm off on a case-by-case basis when you don't want to be notified for any events.

To enable the default alarm setting, do this:

1. In the Day View, choose Options | Preferences.

2. Tap the check box for the Alarm Preset. Set your alarm preference; configure the alarm time, the kind of alarm sound, and how many times the alarm will sound before giving up.

> TIP
>
> *You can try out each of the alarm sounds by selecting them from the list. After you choose a sound, it plays so you can hear what it sounds like.*

3. Tap OK.

Import Alarm Settings

Much of the time, you probably get appointments into your Zire via your PC—you HotSync them in from the Palm Desktop or Outlook. In that case, the rules are different. The Zire keeps whatever alarm settings were assigned on the PC and doesn't use the Preference settings on the Zire. If you want a specific alarm setting, you need to change the alarm setting on the desktop application before HotSyncing or change the alarm on the Zire after you HotSync.

> TIP
>
> *Some folks would like to have two separate sets of alarms for their appointments: one for the Zire and another for their desktop calendar program. If you have a PC and Microsoft Outlook, try Desktop to Go. This alternative conduit enables you to configure the Zire to use a completely independent set of alarms from Outlook.*

Work with the Palm Desktop

If you use the Palm Desktop as the calendar on your desktop PC, you benefit because it looks similar to the version on your Zire. Granted, the Palm Desktop is a lot bigger than your Zire screen and it's in color, but aside from that, you find the modules share a common appearance and that the overall philosophy of the program is similar.

The Windows Date Book

The Date Book in the Windows version of the Palm Desktop uses a few unique control elements—but they're quite intuitive. After you start the Palm Desktop, you can switch to the Date Book by clicking the Date icon on the right side of the screen or by choosing View | Date Book. To change Views, click the tabs at the right edge of the screen. You should see three tabs: Day, Week, and Month.

Use the Day View

The Day View looks similar to the Zire display. Look at Figure 5-3 for an overview of the major elements in this display.

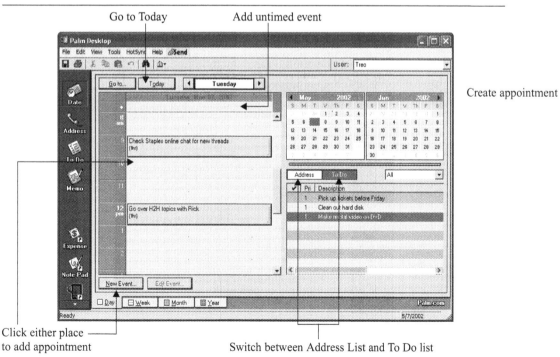

FIGURE 5-3   The Day View combines appointments with either To Dos or Addresses, depending upon how you configure the screen.

The easiest way to double-book a time slot is to click the Time box. A new blank appears to the right of the existing appointment.

You might recall that on the Zire, you can create an appointment by using the Phone Lookup feature—this grabs a name and phone number from the Address Book and places it in a time slot in the Date Book. You can do the same thing in the Palm Desktop. Under the calendar, you can see the To Do List and Address Book minilists. Choose which one you want to see by clicking Address or To Do. Then drag a name (or even a To Do) into a time slot.

Use the Week and Month Views

Both of these Views are quite similar to their Zire counterparts. When in the Week View (seen in Figure 5-4), though, the event blocks work a little differently than you might expect:

- To move an event to a different time, drag it by the event handle.
- To display the Edit Event dialog box and change options like text, time, repeat settings, or the alarm, double-click the event.
- To change the duration of the event, drag its duration handle up or down.

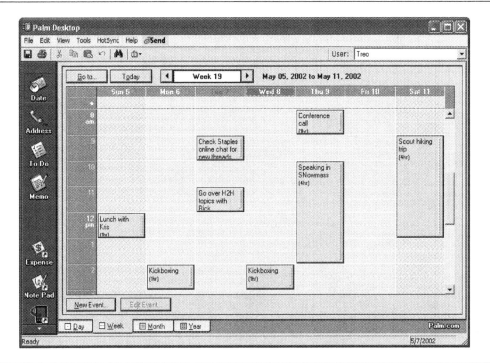

FIGURE 5-4 The Week View enables you to add and edit appointments.

The Month View is a bit more helpful than the one in your Zire. The Month View actually shows you what events are scheduled, not only that you have a mysterious "something" scheduled. You can't edit the events in this View, though. Instead, you can double-click the appropriate day to get to the Day View or add a new event to a specific day by right-clicking the day and choosing New Event from the menu.

Using Outlook

Of course, Microsoft Outlook synchronizes with the Zire just fine, and many people use it instead of the Palm Desktop. We should point out, though, that some people categorize appointments in Outlook. The Zire doesn't let you categorize events in the Date Book, but you can add this capability by upgrading to a HotSync conduit like Chapura's PocketMirror Professional.

Navigating Around Outlook

The Outlook Calendar View is a handy tool for seeing your current and upcoming events. By default, you see today's appointments. To switch to a specific day, click the date you want in the minicalendar (see Figure 5-5). You can also see several days at a time. To do this, click-and-drag a range of days in the minicalendar.

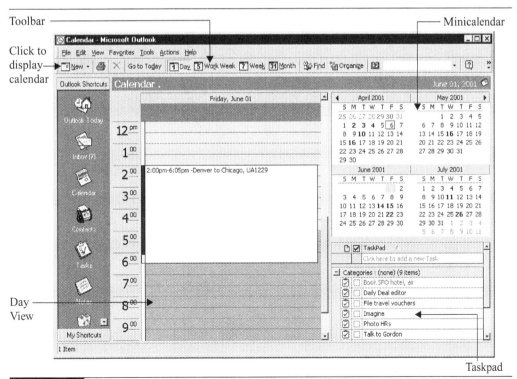

FIGURE 5-5   Many users synchronize with Outlook instead of the Palm Desktop.

The toolbar includes buttons for viewing the work week, an entire week, and a month at a glance. To switch back to a single view of today, you need to click both Day (to switch to a single day view) and then Go To Today (to view the current day).

Tweaking Alarms for the Zire

By default, every Outlook appointment comes with an alarm that sounds 15 minutes before the event. If you create most of your appointments within Outlook, you might end up with alarms you don't want on the Zire after a HotSync. To change the length of the default alarm— or to disable alarms entirely—choose Tools | Options from the Outlook menu and click the Preferences tab. In the Calendar section, edit the Default Reminder option to suit your needs. If you remove the check mark, the alarm is then disabled for new appointments.

Disable alarms

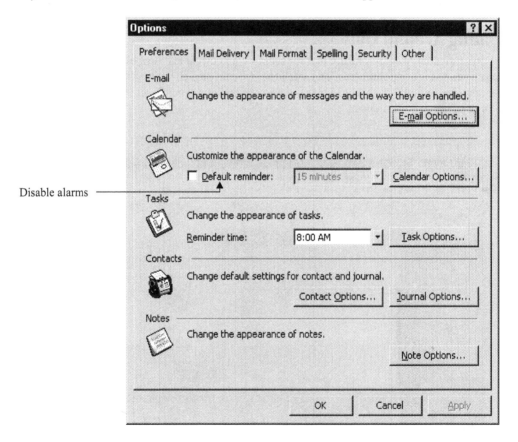

Chapter 6

The Address Book

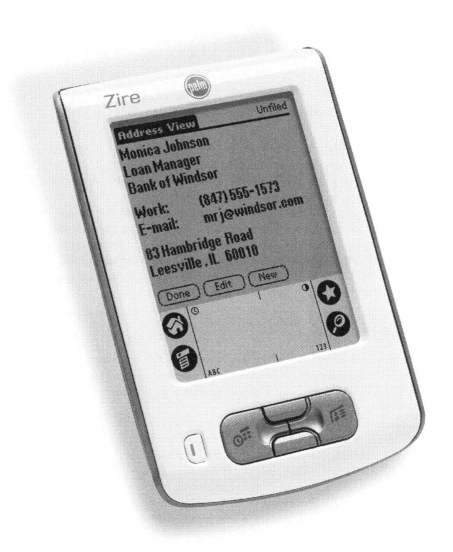

How to...

- View Address Book entries
- Customize the Address List display
- Search for an entry by name
- Search for an entry by keyword
- Create new Address Book entries
- Display a specific phone number in the Address List
- Use the custom fields
- Assign a category to an entry
- Delete Address Book entries
- Use the Windows Address Book
- Use your Zire with Outlook

What's the big deal? It's only an address book. Yes, but as one of the four big "core" applications—the main programs that ship with your Zire—you'll use the Address Book a lot, and the Address Book is an elegant program, designed to get the information you need quickly—perhaps more quickly than any other contact manager on the market.

You can store as many as 10,000 entries—if you know that many people. No matter how many names you add to the list, your Zire never slows down; that's a claim desktop applications simply can't make. In addition, the Address Book isn't really a stand-alone application (though it can be if you want). The Address Book synchronizes with desktop applications like Palm Desktop and Microsoft Outlook. This means you need to create a contact list only once, and then it's maintained on both your PC and your Zire.

View Your Addresses

When you switch to the Address Book, the program displays all the entries in your list onscreen. As you might expect, you can start the Address Book by pressing the Address button on the front of your Zire (it's the one on the right) or tapping the onscreen Address icon in the Applications screen.

As you can see in Figure 6-1, the Zire lists your contacts alphabetically in a view called the Address List. There's room for 11 entries onscreen at one time; the rest appear above or below the screen, depending on where you are within the list. To get around in the Address List, just use the Scroll buttons. Each time you scroll, the Zire moves the list by one complete page of entries.

You can also get around with categories. If your contacts are divided into more than one category, every time you press the Address button, you switch categories. You can cycle through the first page of names in each category by repeatedly pressing the Address Book button.

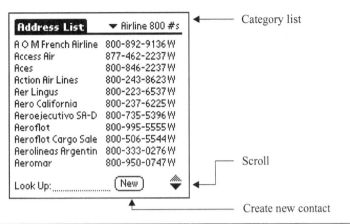

Category list

Scroll

Create new contact

FIGURE 6-1 The Address List is a database of all your contact information.

View by Company Name

For most folks, the default Address List is great. This list displays the entries by name (last, first) and a phone number. If you prefer to work with your contacts according to the company they work with, you can change the Address List.

To change the View mode of the Address List, do this:

1. Display the Address List View.

2. Choose Options | Preferences from the menu.

3. Choose Company, Last Name from the List By list.

4. Tap OK to save your changes.

Notice that after making the change, you can see the company name in the list. If no company is associated with a particular entry, you only see the individual's name, as you did before. You can switch back to the default view at any time.

Find a Specific Name

If you're looking for a specific entry in the Address List, you can simply scroll down until you find it. If you have only a few dozen contacts, that's not so hard. But what if you're like us and your Address List is brimming with over a thousand contacts? Scrolling might take a while, especially if the guy you're looking for is named Nigel Walthers or Earnest Zanthers. That's when you use the Look Up function.

To search for a specific name, start writing the person's last name in the Look Up field at the bottom of the screen. The Address Book adjusts the display as you write; so if you enter the letter **J**, it displays all the names that begin with the letter *J*. If you write **JO**, it narrows the search and shows names that begin with those letters.

Once you start searching, you can keep writing letters until the Zire displays exactly the name you want, or you can write one or two letters and then use the Scroll button to find the name you need. If you want to clear the Look Up field to write in a new name, just press one of the Scroll buttons.

 *If you try writing a letter but your Zire beeps at you, this means no name in the list is spelled with the letter you're trying to add. You've probably misspelled the name.*

Conduct a Detailed Search

You may have noticed that the Look Up field only searches by last name. What happens if you want to find someone, but you can only remember that person's first name or the company where he works? The Look Up field won't do any good.

In this case, use the Find tool. Tap the Find button (shaped like a magnifying glass), enter the word you want to search for, and then tap OK. You get a list of every entry in the Zire with that word—even items from the other applications—as shown in Figure 6-2. The current application is searched first, so make sure you're in the Address Book before you start using the Find tool.

View a Name

Once you locate the name you were looking for, tap on it. You see the Address view, which displays the contact's name, address, and phone numbers, as shown in Figure 6-3.

Create New Entries

To create a new Address List entry on the Zire, tap the New button at the bottom of the screen. From there, start filling in the blanks. Start by writing the last name of the person you're adding.

FIGURE 6-2   The Find tool is a powerful way to locate an entry, even if you don't remember the person's exact name.

When you're ready to move on to the first name, you need to change fields. You can do this in two ways:

- Tap the next field with the stylus and write in the Graffiti area.
- Use the Next Field gesture to move to the next field.

TIP   *The Next Field gesture takes a little practice because it's easy to get the letter* U *by mistake. Although the gesture template shows a curve in the first part of the stroke, you get the best results by going straight down, and then straight up again.*

FIGURE 6-3   The Address Book shows you all the details about the selected individual.

Even though you only see a single line for text in each field, the Address List secretly supports multiple lines of text in each field. If you're entering the company name, for instance, you can use two or more lines to enter all the information you need about the company, department, and so on for the individual. To write multiple lines of text in a field, use the Return gesture to create a new line. You won't see the multiple lines in the Address List, but you can see them when you select the entry and view the Address View.

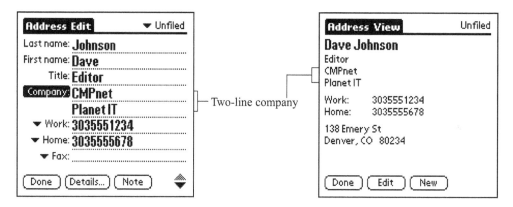

When you've finished adding information about this new person, tap the Done button.

What if you're Canadian, French, or living in some other non-American location? The Zire defaults to address details like city, state, and ZIP code—which may not be appropriate for your locale. The solution is to tap on the Prefs icon in Apps and select Formats from the menu. Then, set the Preset To menu to whatever country you desire.

Use Multiple Phone Numbers

The Address List gives you a few options when you enter contact information. Specifically, you can set what kinds of phone numbers your Zire has for each contact. For one person, you might list a home phone and a pager, while another entry might have a work number and an e-mail address. The Zire keeps track of everything for you.

To control these numbers, tap on the phone number list and choose the desired label. Then, write the number or e-mail address in the field next to the label. You can specify up to five entries for each person in your Address List.

If you're on the ball, you might wonder which of those numbers shows up in the Address List view. Remember, the list shows the name and a phone number for each contact—this means you may not have to open an entry simply to dial a phone number because it's right there in the List view. The answer, though, is that the first phone number you enter into the Edit view is the one that appears in the List view—no matter where it appears in the list of phone numbers.

If you later decide you want a different number to appear in the List view, tap the Details button and select the number label you want from the Show in List menu.

Use Extra Fields

The Address List has plenty of preconfigured fields (like name, company, and phone numbers) for most users, but it's flexible enough also to accommodate the special needs of everyone else. You might want to track birthdays, Web pages, spouse names, or other personal information. If so, you're in luck—four custom fields are at the bottom of the Address Edit view, which you can rename as you like.

To label these four bonus fields into something more useful, do this:

1. Choose the Address Book. Any view will do.

2. Choose Options | Rename Custom Fields from the menu.

3. Select the text on the first line (which should say Custom 1) and write a name for the field. Name the other fields—or as many as you need—in the same way.

4. Tap OK when you finish.

6

Dialing Your Phone with a Zire

Now that you've got hundreds of phone numbers stored on your Zire, it's better equipped to place phone calls for you than the speed dial feature on your desktop phone. If you don't mind investing in a gadget called the Parlay Autodialer, you can point your PDA at your phone and automatically dial phone numbers.

The Autodialer is a small infrared receiver that plugs into your telephone (sort of like an answering machine) and intercepts beams from your Zire. Beam an Address Book entry toward your phone, and it dials the associated phone number. It's as simple as that.

If you change the Zire's preferences so a single upstroke across the display starts the beaming process (that's something you can configure in the Prefs program, explained in Chapter 4), dialing is effortless: just find an Address Book entry, point your PDA at the Autodialer, and beam. Pick up your handset or turn on the speakerphone to complete the call.

Once you create labels for these fields, you can find them at the bottom of the list of contact info in the Address Edit view.

The custom fields are global. This means you can't have different custom fields for each entry or even for each category. Once named, the custom fields apply to all entries in the Address List. You needn't fill them out for every entry, though.

Assign Categories

Your new contact can easily get lost within a sea of names and addresses if you aren't careful. With only a few names to manage, this isn't a big deal. But what if you have 500 or 1,000 contacts in your Address List? This is when categories could come in handy.

Choose a Category

As you might remember from Chapter 2, categories are simply a way of organizing your data more logically into groups you frequently use. To assign a contact to a specific category, do this:

1. From the Address Edit screen, tap Details. The Address Entry Details dialog box should appear.

2. Tap the Category List and choose the category name you want to assign to this contact.

3. Tap OK to close the dialog box.

Of course, you needn't assign a category if you don't want to do so. By default, new contacts are placed in the Unfiled category.

Edit and Delete Addresses

In this fast-paced world, a contact once entered in an address book isn't likely to stay that way for long. You may need to update an address, phone number, or e-mail address, or delete the entry entirely.

To edit an entry, all you must do is find the entry in the Address List and tap it. You're taken to the Address View where you can see the existing information. Then, tap on the screen and the display changes to the Address Edit screen, which you can change to suit your needs.

If you have a contact you simply don't need anymore, you can delete it from the Zire to save memory and reduce data clutter. To delete a contact, do this:

1. Choose the entry from the Address List.

2. Choose Record | Delete Address from the menu.

NOTE

If you check the box marked Save Archive Copy on PC, a copy of this entry is preserved in the Palm Desktop in archive form. In general, you probably needn't archive your data, but it lets you restore deleted data in a crisis. To get at archived data on the desktop, start the Palm Desktop and switch to the Address Book. Choose File | Open Archive... from the menu.

Create and Beam Your Business Card

As mentioned in Chapter 4, one of the coolest things about taking your Zire to meetings and trade shows is the capability to beam your personal information into other peoples' PDAs. This is a lot easier and more convenient than exchanging a business card. Heck, a paper business card? That's so…'80s! Use your Zire instead.

Before you can beam your personal information around, though, you need to create a business card. That's not hard to do. Find your own personal information in the Address List (or, if you haven't done this yet, create an entry for yourself). After you select your card and you can see your personal information on the Address View screen, choose Record | Select Business Card from the menu.

From here on, you can beam your card to others either by choosing Record | Beam Business Card from the Address List menu or, more simply, by holding the Address List button down for two seconds.

 *Is your Address List entry selected as your business card? It's easy to tell. On the Address View, you can see an icon representing a Rolodex page at the top of the screen, to the right of the title.*

Work with the Palm Desktop

The Palm Desktop obviously has its own counterpart to the Address Book found in the Zire. Using the Palm Desktop, you can not only create, edit, and refer to entries on your PC, but you can also put them to use in ways unavailable on the PDA itself. Next, we look at the Palm Desktop.

Using the Address Book in the Palm Desktop is a radically different experience than using the Zire. In most respects, it's better because the larger desktop screen, keyboard, and mouse enable you to enter and use the data in a more flexible way. After you start the Palm Desktop, you can switch to the Address Book by clicking the Address icon on the right side of the screen or by choosing View | Address Book (see Figure 6-4).

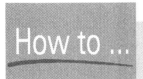 **Create an Address Book Entry**

In summary, here's how you can create entries in the Address Book:

1. Press the Address Book button on your Zire to switch to that app.
2. Tap the New button on the bottom of the Address List view.
3. Enter all the information to create an entry for the person in question.
4. Tap the Details button and assign the entry to a category and tap OK.

6

Address list   Change category   Address details

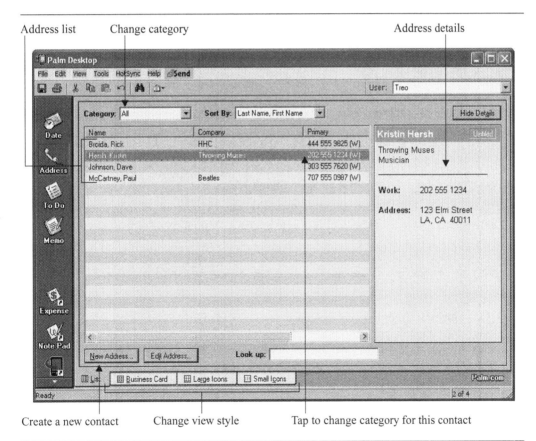

Create a new contact   Change view style   Tap to change category for this contact

FIGURE 6-4   The Address Book looks sparse, but has more features than the Zire itself.

The Address Book interface enables you to see both the Address List and Address View simultaneously. To see a specific record's contents, click it in the list, and the information then appears in the column on the right.

 *You can print a detailed address book based on your Zire contacts by choosing File | Print. The address book is nicely formatted.*

Create and Edit Entries

Some of the most dramatic differences in the Address Book appear when you create and use the Address Book. Remember these notes:

- To create a new entry, click the New button at the bottom of the screen or double-click a blank spot in the Address List.

- The Edit and New dialog boxes allow you to enter the same information as on the Zire. The dialog box also has a list box for specifying the category and a check box to make the entry private.

- To specify which phone number will appear in the Address List, click the radio button to the left of the appropriate phone number.

- To edit an existing entry, either double-click the entry in the Address List or its equivalent in the Address View on the right.

- You can also change the custom fields on the Palm Desktop. To do that, choose Tools | Options and click the Address tab.

Import Contacts into the Palm Desktop

If you have a history with another contact manager, you could have dozens or even hundreds of names and addresses that should be copied over to the Palm Desktop to be synchronized with the Zire. Thankfully, the Palm Desktop makes importing all those contacts possible with a minimum of fuss. All you need is a contact manager capable of saving its data in either a comma-separated (CSV) or a tab-separated (TSV) format. To import your data from another program, do this:

1. In your old contact manager, find the menu option to export your data in either CSV or TSV format. If the program gives you an option to remap your data as it's saved, don't worry. We'll map it properly as it's imported into the Palm Desktop. Save the exported data to a file on your hard disk. Make a note of where you save this file because you need to find it again in about two steps.

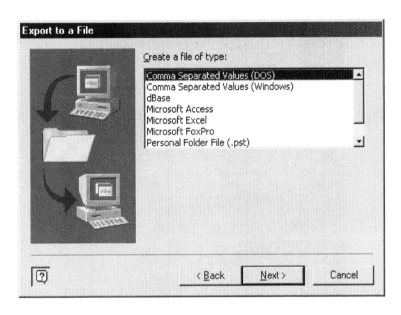

2. In the Palm Desktop, choose File | Import. The Import dialog box should appear.

3. Select the file you just created with the old contact manager. You may have to choose the proper file extension (like CSV or TSV) from the Type Of File list box to see the file you created. Choose Open.

4. Now you see a Specify Import Fields dialog box, as shown in Figure 6-5. This is the hardest part of the process and the one part that isn't terribly automated. Here's the deal: the data in a typical contact entry includes items like name, phone numbers, and address. However, those fields won't be in the same order in any two contact management programs, so you need to help the Palm Desktop put the old data in the right fields as it imports. To map the fields properly, drag each field on the left (which is the Palm Desktop) until it's lined up with the proper field on the right (which represents the old program). Line up last name with last name, for instance, and match phone numbers, e-mail addresses, and any other important fields. If you don't want to import a certain field, deselect its check box.

TIP *You can use the arrows to cycle forward through the database and make sure you assigned the fields properly.*

5. When you finish lining up the fields, click the OK button.

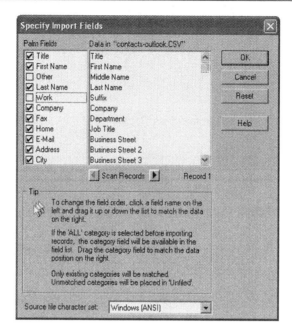

FIGURE 6-5   Carefully rearrange the fields in the Specify Import Fields dialog box so your old data is imported properly into the Palm Desktop.

If you did everything right, you should see your contacts in the Palm Desktop. Any newly imported entries are highlighted. If you messed something up, all isn't lost. Simply delete all your records and try to import your contacts file again.

Using Outlook

As we mentioned in Chapter 5, Outlook is a perfectly good alternative to the Palm Desktop. To see your contacts in Outlook, start by clicking the Contacts icon in the Outlook Shortcut bar. Outlook should switch to the Contacts view, and then you see a complete list of your names and addresses.

You can view your contacts in many ways. That's good, because if you're anything like us, you have hundreds of entries—and sorting through them can be like finding a virtual needle in a digital haystack. To see your options, click the Organize button in the Outlook toolbar. The Organize pane should open. Click Using Views, and you can experiment with arranging your contacts by category, by company, or nearly any other way imaginable.

To find a contact quickly from any view in Outlook, type the person's name in the Find A Contact field on the Outlook toolbar and press ENTER. *Outlook displays a list of names that matches your criteria or, if only one name appears, displays its entry.*

Working with Your Zire

Outlook can hold a wealth of information, but it's important for you to understand the Zire's limitations when synchronizing to Outlook. Not all the fields in Outlook get transferred to the Zire because there simply aren't enough fields. Specifically, the limitations in the HotSync from Outlook to the Zire are the following:

■ By default, only the business address is stored on the Zire. You can upgrade to other HotSync conduits that let you synchronize the personal address. Specifically, try PocketMirror Professional or Intellisync.

■ Work, Home, Fax, Mobile, and E-mail are typically the only contact fields transferred to the Zire. If you create a contact with alternative fields, like Business 2 or alternative e-mail addresses, Zire tries to include these entries, space permitting.

■ None of the data from the Details tab is stored on the Zire.

This illustration should help you see how the Zire's Address Book entries correlate to Outlook:

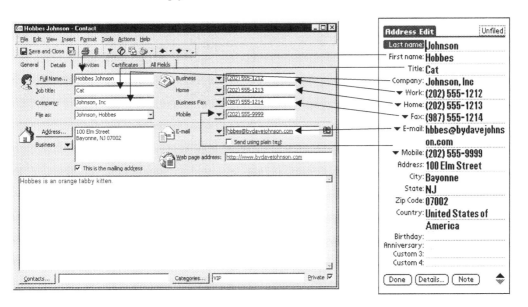

Where to Find It

Web Site	Address	What's There
Chapura	www.chapura.com	PocketMirror Professional and KeyContacts
Pumatech	www.pumatech.com	Intellisync
Synchroscan	www.pda2phone.com	Parlay Autodialer

Chapter 7

The To Do List

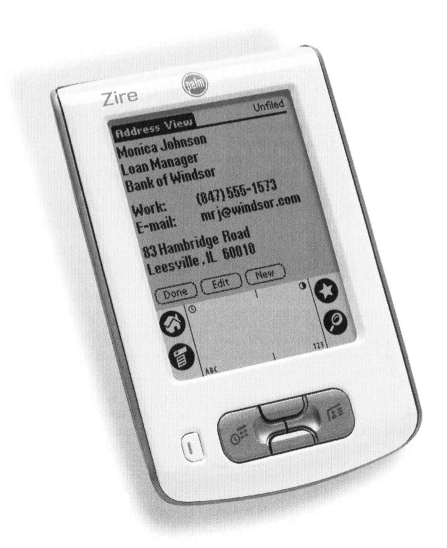

How to...

- Create new To Dos
- Create a To Do based on an Address Book entry
- Prioritize your To Dos
- Add notes to your To Dos
- Edit To Dos from the List view
- Customize the To Do List view
- Beam To Dos to others
- Use the Palm Desktop for Windows
- Export To Dos to Word and Excel
- Using Outlook with the Zire

The To Do List is admittedly one of the simplest of the built-in programs, but don't let that fool you. There's a lot of convenience under the hood. What good is this little program? Well, think of it this way: would you be more organized if you actually carried a list of things you needed to do—big and small—with you all the time? Finish a task and cross it off the list for a sense of immediate gratification, or, think of something you need to do while you're away from the office and add it immediately to the Zire, knowing the entry will be added to your PC's master To Do List as soon as you HotSync. The To Do List is a way to take charge of all the little things that make up your daily agenda.

View the To Do List

You might have noticed there's no button on the front the Zire to start the To Do List. Start the program by tapping its icon on the Application screen.

> TIP
>
> *If you use the To Do List more often than, say, the Address Book, you can reprogram the Address Book button to start the To Do List. Open the Prefs app and choose Buttons from the menu to set this preference.*

As you can see in Figure 7-1, the Zire lists your To Dos in a fairly straightforward list that you can use to see what tasks you have coming up or, in some cases, past due (you might want to take care of those pretty soon). The Zire screen has room for 11 entries at one time; the rest appear "above" or "below" the screen, depending on where you are within the To Do List. Getting around is easy. Simply scroll down to see more names, either with the onscreen scroll arrows or the Scroll buttons on the Zire's case.

Each time you scroll, the Zire moves the list by one complete page. This means that if you scroll down, the bottom entry on the page becomes the top entry after scrolling.

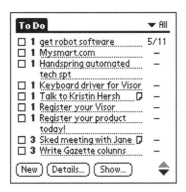

FIGURE 7-1   The To Do List displays all of your pending tasks.

7

Another way to get around is by using the categories. If your tasks are divided into more than one category, every time you press the To Do button, you switch categories. You can cycle through the first page of tasks in each category by repeatedly pressing this button.

Create a To Do

To add a To Do, just start writing in the Graffiti area. The text appears automatically in a brand new To Do entry.

 *If you want to create a task with a specific priority, tap on a To Do entry that has the priority you want and tap New. The new To Do takes the priority of the previously selected task, saving you the trouble of choosing a priority later.*

While most tasks can be summarized in only one line of text, there's no reasonable limit to how long you can make a To Do entry. If you need more than one line of text to describe your task, you can use the Enter gesture to get the Zire to display a new blank line in the same To Do.

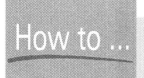 **The Agenda Shows To Dos**

You can view your To Do items in the Date Book. The Agenda view lets you see all of today's appointments and upcoming To Dos at a glance, all on the same screen. See Chapter 5.

Remember, though, creating multiline To Dos might make it hard for you to read your tasks later, as you can see here:

Instead of making long, multiline tasks, we recommend you add a note to your task instead (explained later in this chapter).

Add Some Details

Once you finish entering the name of the task, tap elsewhere on the screen to save the entry. If you prefer, you can add additional information, like a priority, category, and due date. You don't have to enter any of these special settings, but using them enables you to track your tasks with greater accuracy. Here's what you need to do:

1. Select the task you want to edit by tapping the name of the To Do.

2. Tap the Details button.

3. Tap a number to represent the priority of your task. You can select any number from one to five (the lower the number, the higher the priority).

4. Choose a category from the Category List.

5. Choose a due date from the Due Date List. You can choose to make a task due today, tomorrow, or in a week, or you can choose a date directly from the Calendar dialog box.

6. Tap OK to save your changes to the task.

Friends Are a Chore

It's true! Having friends and coworkers can be actual work. Suppose you need to meet with Ed Grimpley from accounting sometime this week to talk about why you've gone through 18 mouse pads in the space of one week. You don't have an appointment in your calendar; you'd rather pop in sometime when it's convenient. The To Do List is your answer. Create a new To Do and choose Options | Phone Lookup from the menu. Find Ed in the Phone Number Lookup dialog box and tap Add. What you get is Ed's name and phone number in the To Do entry. It's a handy way to remind yourself to call someone without setting up a rigid appointment in the Date Book.

While you can make a task almost any length, most people find it's better to keep the To Do short, and add a note. To add a note to a To Do, select your To Do, tap the Details button, and then tap Note.

7

Work with the List View

When you switch to the To Do List, all of your existing tasks arranged onscreen, usually in order of importance (as determined by the priority number assigned to each To Do). As you can see in Figure 7-2, six elements are associated with each task:

- **Check box**   If you complete a task, you can indicate it's done by tapping the check box. That places a check mark in the task. Depending on how you configured the To Do Preferences, the entry either disappears or remains onscreen, but is marked as done.

- **Priority**   Not everything is the most important thing on your task list. If you want to arrange your tasks by importance or urgency, use the priority numbers, from 1 through 5. Tap the number to get a list of all the priority choices.

We recommend that you use priority numbers for your tasks—they help you sort through the clutter of your various To Dos and determine what's really important from one day to the next.

To Do or Appointment?

We know what you're thinking—if you can assign due dates to items in the To Do List, why bother with appointments? Or, from the other perspective, why use To Dos if you have the Date Book? That's a good question. We use the To Do List whenever we have tasks that need doing by a certain date—but not at a certain time of day. If it requires a time slot, we put it in the Date Book. So, stuff like "buy lemons" and "finish Chapter 12" (hint, hint, Rick . . .) are To Dos. "Meet with Laura for lunch at 11:30" is a Date Book entry. There's also the matter of alarms: your Zire has an alarm for appointments, but not for To Dos.

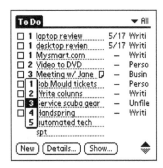

FIGURE 7-2 The To Do List lets you modify your tasks without tapping the Details button.

- **To Do description** You can edit the description of the task by tapping in this field and editing the existing text.

- **Note icon** If you already created a note for the task, you can read the note or edit it by tapping the icon to the right of the To Do name field. If no note already exists, you can add one by selecting the task and choosing Record | Attach Note from the menu.

- **Due date** You might have tasks that need to be accomplished by a specific date. If this is the case, use the final column. If a dash is in that slot, this means you haven't yet assigned a due date. Tap it and choose a date. You can also change the due date in the same way.

- **Category** Change the category to which a task is assigned by tapping the category column and choosing the desired category from the list.

Some of these columns aren't displayed by default—to enable them, tap the Show button and choose the columns you want to appear in the To Do Preferences dialog box.

Change the View Options

If you're anything like us (and that could be a very, very bad thing, if you know what we mean), you may be perfectly happy with the default look of the To Do List. It's easy to modify, though. Tap the Show button and you see the To Do Preferences dialog box. Here are your options:

Sorting Options

The first item you encounter in the Preferences dialog box is a Sort By list. This determines the way the To Do List shows the tasks onscreen.

- **Priority, Due Date**   This groups all the priority 1 tasks first, then priority 2, and so on. Within each priority group, the earliest deadlines are listed first, and no deadline tasks are listed last. This option works best if you need to work on tasks with the highest priority, and due dates aren't particularly important to you.

- **Due Date, Priority**   This selection arranges all the tasks by due date, with the soonest due dates listed first and no due dates listed last. If several tasks have the same due date, they're listed by priority order. This is probably the best display option for most people—it lists your tasks with the ones due soonest at the top of the page and, within each due date, you can see the top priorities arranged first.

- **Category, Priority**   Arranges your tasks by category. The categories are arranged in alphabetical order. If you have more than one task in a given category, they're arranged in priority order within the category. Use this category if seeing tasks visually arranged into different categories—like work and personal—is more important for you than arranging them by due date or category.

- **Category, Due Date**   This selection also arranges your tasks by category, and the categories are arranged in alphabetical order. If you have more than one task in a given category, they're arranged by due date within the category. Soonest deadlines appear first, and no due date tasks are placed last within each category.

Use Filters to Customize the Display

The next section in the To Do Preferences dialog box controls what kinds of tasks are displayed onscreen. Actually, that's not true, but we're trying to apply some logic to the way Zire chooses to group the items on this screen. Here's what each of these three items does:

- **Show Completed Items**   As you check off tasks you complete, slowly but surely they clutter up your screen unless you do something about them. If you uncheck this option, completed items are hidden. If you need to see items you have completed, simply check Show Completed Items and they reappear.

If you hide completed tasks in this way, they're not deleted—they still take up memory on the Zire. See later in this chapter to find out how to delete old To Dos.

- **Show Only Due Items**   If you're only concerned about tasks due today, check this item. Any tasks with a due date after today disappear from the screen and only reappear on the day they're due.

 *Be careful with this option because it hides To Dos from the screen that aren't due today, regardless of priority. It's easy to get caught off guard by a major deadline this way.*

■ **Record Completion Date**   This interesting little feature changes the due date of a completed item to the date it was completed. If you didn't assign a due date to a task, the completion date becomes the due date. In this way, you can track what day you completed each of your tasks.

 *This option overwrites the due date with the completion date. You can't get the original due date back, even if you uncheck the task or turn off the Record Completion Date option.*

Modify the Task Columns

As you probably already saw, you can tweak the data the To Do List shows you for each task in the list. That tweaking occurs here, in the last three options of the To Do Preferences dialog box. Your To Do List can look sparse, highly decorated, or anything in between by changing the Show options:

■ **Show Due Dates**   The due date format is day/month, which takes some getting used to. If you don't assign a due date to a task, you see a dash instead. On the To Do List, if you tap a due date you see a list for changing the date.

■ **Show Priorities**   This displays the priority to the left of the To Do name. The priority can be adjusted by tapping the number on the To Do List view.

■ **Show Categories**   The category of the task appears on the right edge of the To Do List view if you use this option. You can assign a category to an unfiled To Do (or change the category of a previously filed entry) by tapping the category name on the To Do List view.

White Goes with Everything

Dave: I'm not so sure about my Zire's white front. It's so plain looking, I can't help but wish I could slap multicolored faceplates on, like you can do with some mobile phones. Or how about a nice *Simpsons* faceplate? That would be cool. A faceplate that glowed in the dark would be nice too. Palm just doesn't seem to have a sense of style. Then again, you like to actually clip your PDA to your belt, so why am I even asking you about this?

Rick: Hey, pal, when women see that Zire on my belt, they positively throw themselves at me. I'm not surprised you don't like the Zire's white veneer, as you usually dress in black from head to head. (How *is* high school these days, anyway?) I think the Zire looks downright cute—much sleeker and shinier than the Palms of old. In fact, given the price, I wouldn't have expected much in the way of looks at all, but the Zire has a kind of kitchen-appliance cool.

7

Delete Old To Dos

For most people, To Dos are not like diamonds—they don't last forever. After you check off a task that says "pick up a loaf of bread," how long do you need a record of having accomplished that goal? That's why your Zire provides a method of removing tasks you no longer want. The Zire offers you two ways to eliminate tasks:

- ■ **Delete them one at a time** If you need to delete only one To Do, tap in the To Do to select it. Now choose Record | Delete Item from the menu, and the To Do is gone forever.

- ■ **Delete a whole bunch at once** If you use the To Do List a lot and develop a back list of dozens or hundreds of completed tasks occasionally, axing them one at a time could become a full-time job. Instead, purge them. A *purge* deletes all completed tasks, so be sure you want to do this. To purge your To Do List, choose Record | Purge from the menu. The Purge dialog box appears, asking if you really want to delete your completed To Dos. Tap OK.

 *If you want to preserve a copy of your completed tasks, check Save Archive Copy on PC, and then load the archive into the Palm Desktop (choose File | Open Archive from the menu) when you need to refer to the entries.*

Share Your To Dos

Delegation is the key to successful management. At least that's what we've been told. We don't actually supervise anyone, but it sounds like solid business advice, nonetheless. You can use your Zire as a solid delegation tool by beaming tasks to other people. Just like in other applications, you can beam a single item or all the items in a specific category. Here's the skinny:

- **Beam a single To Do** To beam one To Do to someone, choose a task by tapping inside the To Do name. Then choose Record | Beam Item from the menu.

- **Beam a whole bunch of items** You can beam an entire category's worth of To Dos at once. To do this, switch the current view to show the category you want to beam. Choose a category from the list at the top right of the screen. Then choose Record | Beam Category from the menu.

Work with the Palm Desktop

Who says the only place you can enter To Dos is on your Zire? Not us! The Palm Desktop has a module dedicated to tracking your tasks. Using the Palm Desktop, you can enter To Dos and have them appear on your Zire when you're away from your desk.

The To Do List's interface is a bit more spacious than the one in your Zire, as you can see in Figure 7-3. As a result, the Palm Desktop pulls off a cool trick—it displays both the list itself and the contents of the Details dialog box onscreen simultaneously. Click a To Do, and the details on the right automatically update to show you more information about the particular task you selected.

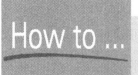 **Create Tasks on Your Handheld**

We've talked a lot about To Dos, so here's a summary of how to create tasks on your Zire:

1. Tap the To Do button on the Zire's Application screen.

2. Start writing in the Graffiti area—this creates a new To Do.

3. Tap the Details button.

If you want to, assign a priority, category, and due date on the Details dialog box. Tap OK to close this dialog box.

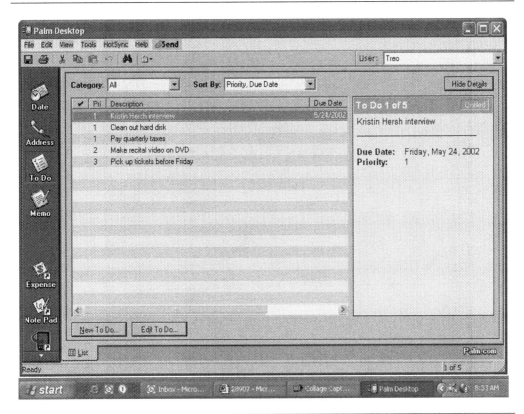

7

FIGURE 7-3   You can see the details on any To Do by clicking the appropriate description on the left side of the screen.

Using Outlook

If you're an Outlook user, you probably already know that Zire's To Do items become tasks in Outlook. In fact, that's pretty much all you need to know to use Outlook with your Zire. To see your To Dos in Outlook, click the Tasks icon in the Outlook Shortcuts bar. The tasks are also displayed in the Taskbar section of the Calendar.

When you mark a task as completed in Outlook, it isn't deleted. To reduce clutter and save disk space, you might want to delete tasks occasionally. To do this, right-click a completed task and choose Delete from the menu.

Turn To Dos into Appointments

Your Zire understands there's a tight relationship between your calendar and your To Do tasks. Switch to the Date Book in the Palm Desktop and you'll find the right side of the screen has a window for displaying either addresses or To Dos. Click the To Do box to show To Dos; click Address to return to the Phone Number Lookup mode. What good is that? Well, you can actually grab a To Do and drag-and-drop it into a calendar appointment. That lets you turn a task into a bona fide appointment. You can't go the other way, though, and turn an appointment into a task.

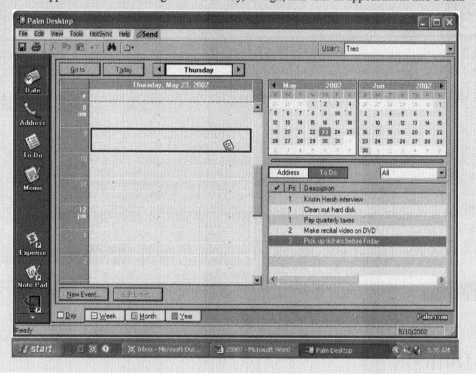

Understanding Task Priorities

The Zire and Outlook use two slightly different ways of assigning priority to tasks and To Dos. Thankfully, the two systems work together and are easy to figure out. Use this guide to correlate the Zire and Outlook systems:

Zire	Outlook
1	High
2	Normal
3	Normal
4	Normal
5	Low

A Better To Do List

We hear what you're saying (figuratively, not literally, of course—those voices we hear are actually the dog talking). The To Do List simply isn't powerful enough. Well, there's a great alternative called ToDo Plus (from Hands High Software at **www.handshigh.com**).

ToDo Plus enables you to attach drawings to your tasks, use templates to customize your entries, add alarms, and much more. One of the most interesting features is a comprehensive set of filters that lets you display your tasks in a variety of useful ways. Give it a try, and you may never want to use the built-in To Do List again.

Chapter 8

The Memo Pad and Note Pad

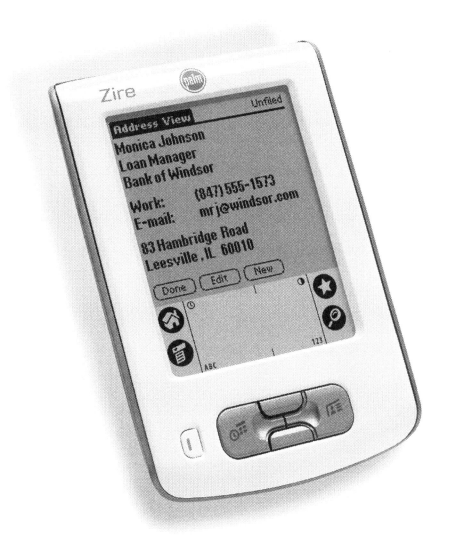

How to...

- View the Memo List
- Create new memos
- Cut, copy, and paste text in a memo
- Assign categories to memos
- Customize the appearance of memos in the Memo list
- Beam memos
- Make memos private
- Delete old memos
- Import text files into Windows memos
- Use memos in other Windows applications

As you've already seen, applications like the Date Book, Address Book, and To Do List let you attach long notes to your entries. A note in the Address Book, for instance, enables you to list directions to the person's house, the names of all their kids, or ten reasons not to visit them on Thanksgiving. But there's also an application designed to do nothing but create notes. These memos can be memory joggers, information you need to take on a trip, or anything not explicitly connected to an address, an appointment, or a to-do. The Memo Pad is your chance, in a sense, to color outside the lines and leave yourself any kind of message you want. And speaking of coloring, you can use the Note Pad to draw, sketch, doodle, and write notes with "digital ink." We'll talk about both of these apps in this chapter. Let's start with the Memo Pad.

Where's the Memo Pad Button?

Like with the To Do List, neither the Memo Pad nor the Note Pad has its own button on the Zire. Instead, you can launch the apps directly from the Zire's Applications screen or reassign one of the programmable buttons to start these programs. To do that, open the Prefs app and choose Buttons from the menu to set your preference (see Chapter 9).

Viewing the Memo Pad

The Memo Pad has two views: the Memo List (which is, not surprisingly, a list of all the memos you created) and the Memo view, which shows you the contents of whatever memo you select from the Memo List. When you start the Memo Pad, it always starts in the Memo List view. As you can see in Figure 8-1, the Zire displays each of your memos in a list, with the first line of the memo visible as a kind of title that lets you know what's inside. Getting around is easy—just scroll up or down to see more memos.

FIGURE 8-1   The Memo List displays all of your memos.

Cool Things to Do with the Memo Pad

Do you know what surprises us? Lots of things, actually. Dave is surprised Rick has no appreciation for the fine arts—specifically, bands like *Pink Floyd*, the *Velvet Underground*, Kristin Hersh, and the *Throwing Muses*. (Inexplicably, Rick has an entirely different definition of "fine arts.")

More to the point, we're surprised at how many people can't seem to come up with good uses for the Memo Pad. They let it languish while they use the Address Book and Date Book all the time. To help you fully realize the potential of this cool little application, here are some helpful suggestions for how to use the Memo Pad:

- **A "Million Dollar Idea" memo**   Create a memo with a header that says Million Dollar Ideas. No matter when or where you come up with one of those incredibly amazing ideas to help you retire before you turn 50, pull out your Zire and jot it down.

- **Trade show category**   Got a lot of booths to visit at next month's lawn care trade show? Create a category and put all the memos for that event in the category. As you walk the show floor, you can reference your notes about the show in one easy-to-find set of memos.

- **Stored passwords**   This one is dangerous, so make sure you make it private, but if you have a lot of passwords you routinely need—for your Web sites, computer logons, and that kind of thing—you can store them all in one place in a memo for passwords. Note, we have to reiterate this is kind of dangerous—if your Zire is stolen, you can give all your passwords away if they're not protected properly. We won't even admit to writing it down if questioned in court.

■ **Meeting notes**   Take notes during a meeting and beam the memo to others when the meeting is over.

■ **A "Phone Messages" memo**   Name a memo Phone Messages and when you check voice mail, jot down the notes in your Zire in this memo. If you're diligent about this, you won't end up with a million yellow stickies all over your desk after each VM-checking session. Also, names and phone numbers will be in your Zire where you need them, not splayed out all over your desk.

Creating New Memos

Sure, there's a New button at the bottom of the Memo List—but you don't need to use it. Just start writing in the Graffiti area, and your Zire automatically creates a new memo.

The memo can be as long as you want, up to 4,000 characters, or about 500 words. That should suit your needs most of the time. You can include blank lines and divide your memo into paragraphs—anything you need to make it logical and readable. Think of it as a very, very basic word processor.

 *You can't name your memos in the sense that you can save files on the PC with a specific filename, but the first line of the memo is what appears in the Memo List. To keep things neat and organized, you can write a brief description of the memo on the top line and start the memo itself on the next line.*

Using Editing Tools

The familiar cut, copy, and paste tools are available in every Zire app, but nowhere are they more important than in the Memo Pad, where you're likely to be writing more than a sentence or two. Remember, you don't have to create text from scratch all the time. Using these edit tools, you can move text from other applications and rearrange it to suit your needs.

Suppose, for example, you previously had a Date Book appointment that read

```
Meeting with Ted
```

Within that appointment, you might have created a note that looked like this:

```
Discuss performance review
Get feedback on budget for 2Q
Agree on approach for marketing plan
```

If you want to have a record of your meeting with Ted, take notes in a memo. Open the appointment note and select the three lines of text from the note. With the text selected, choose Edit | Copy from the menu (or you can use the Command gesture and write **C**). Then switch to the Memo Pad, create a new memo, and paste the text into the memo using Edit | Paste (or COMMAND-P using the Graffiti shortcut).

Memo Pad Assistants

Many tools can enhance the experience of creating long notes in the Memo Pad. Here are a few examples you might want to try.

A pair of programs—*TextPlus* and *WordComplete*—can suggest common words as you write. Even before a word is complete, by offering likely options for what you might be writing, either of these apps can significantly reduce the time you spend creating text in the Memo Pad.

MultiClipHack expands the Zire's clipboard. It keeps track of your last 16 cut and copy operations and it allows you to pick them from a drop-down menu to insert in your memo as you write.

After pasting the text into the memo, you can use it as your agenda items and insert notes as needed, giving you a complete record of the meeting. When you HotSync your Zire, you can paste that data into Word or some other application and generate a formal report.

Assigning Categories

After you accumulate a few memos, you might find the Memo List view getting a bit crowded. Clean it up with the Zire's ever-helpful category filing system. Assign a category like this:

1. Create a new memo.

2. Tap the Details button. The Memo Details dialog box appears.

3. Choose a category from the Category list.

4. Tap OK to close the Memo Details dialog box.

Arranging Memos in the Memo List

Computer users are, for the most part, fanatical organizers. Those geeks tend to spend hours straightening up the Desktop so icons appear in exactly the right place when the computer starts each morning. We know you're not that fanatical, but you might want to organize your memos. This isn't pointless busy work: if you need to open the same memo over and over, having the memo appear at the top of the list whenever you open the Memo List can help. At the very least, we're sure you'll want to understand how to take control of the way memos appear onscreen.

Peering into Madness: Dave's and Rick's Memos

Dave: I have a Memo Pad category called Lists. In this category, I have a bunch of memos I refer to all the time. I have a list of movies—whenever I think of a film I want to rent, I add it to the list. Then, when I go to **Netflix.com**, I can add it to my queue. I also have a Songs memo where I can jot down the names of songs I hear on the radio that I might want to download from an MP3 service. I have a list called meals—things I'd like to eat—that I can refer to when I go grocery shopping and get the appropriate ingredients. Finally, I have a Top 10 list. When I think of a funny Top 10 topic—like "Restaurants you won't want to eat at" or "Reasons to own a Zire"—I jot it down so I have something funny to start a speaking engagement.

Rick: I compile similar lists of books I want to read, movies I want to rent, and wines my wife and I have tried and liked. I also use memos to jot down business ideas and any other brainstorms I don't want to forget.

When you add memos to the Memo List, by default, the newest ones always appear at the end of the list. The default order of Memo List entries is essentially chronological, with the oldest entries at the top and the newest ones at the bottom.

It's a little more complicated than that, though. You can specify the sort order of memos by choosing Options | Preferences. You get two choices:

- **Manual** This is the default mode your Zire uses out of the box. New memos are added to the bottom of the list, but you can actually drag and drop memos to different positions in the list. Suppose you have a frequently used memo you want to appear at the top of the screen. Tap and hold the stylus on the entry, and then drag the stylus up to the position where you want it to appear. You should see a line move with the stylus, indicating where the memo will land if you release the stylus.

- **Alphabetic** This option sorts all entries into alphabetical order. If you select this option, the drag-and-drop method of moving memos won't work unless you revert to the manual method.

Blank Lines for Emphasis

Here's a trick you can try if you think the Memo List is too cluttered. If you use the manual ordering method and arrange your memos in a specific order in a near-fanatical way, you might be bothered by the fact that memo number 4 is "touching" memo number 5. Rick, for instance, is adamant about not eating his mashed potatoes if they come in contact with his peas. Maybe you suffer from the same kind of problem with your Zire.

Try this: Create a new memo with a blank first line. You have to enter at least one character on the second line because the Zire doesn't let you create a completely blank memo. Close the memo and you see you've made a new memo with a blank header. Drag this memo between two memos you want separated and voilà: you've found a way to separate memos.

8

Working with Your Memos

You have the same 500-word limit on writing memos as you have with notes in other parts of the Zire suite of applications. That's plenty of space to write, as long as you're not trying to draft your autobiography (for that, see Chapter 11 for info on office suites).

Beaming Memos

You can send a memo or a group of memos to another PDA owner just as easily as beaming any other kind of information. Here's how:

- **Beam one memo**   To beam a memo, you need to tap on the memo you want to beam—this displays the memo in the Memo view. Then choose Record | Beam from the menu. That's all there is to it.

- **Beam a bunch of memos**   To beam more than one memo, they all must be in the same category. Make sure you're in the Memo List view and switch to the category you want to beam. Then choose Record | Beam Category from the menu.

Make a Memo Private

If you have private information stored in a memo, you can easily hide specific memos from prying eyes. The procedure is essentially the same as with other Zire applications. Do this:

1. In the Memo List, select a memo by tapping it.

2. Tap the Details button. You see the To Memo Details dialog box.

3. Tap the Private box to add a check mark. Now the entry is marked as private. Tap OK and you'll see this dialog box:

4. Tap OK to close the dialog box.

The memo probably isn't hidden yet—you still have one more step to go. To make your memo disappear, you need to enable the Private Records feature in the Security app. For details on how to do this, see Chapter 9.

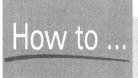 **Create New Memos**

Working with the Memo Pad is a snap. In summary, here's what you need to do to create memos:

1. Tap the Memo Pad icon on your Zire.

2. Start writing in the Graffiti area to create a new memo.

3. Tap the Details button and assign your new memo to a specific category.

4. Tap the Done button to close your new memo.

5. Drag the memo to put it in a specific place in the Memo List.

Deleting Memos

No matter how much you like your memos, eventually you may need to delete some. To delete a memo, tap the memo you want to delete. Then choose Record | Delete Memo from the menu. The memo is then deleted from your Zire. If you prefer, you can save a backup of this memo to the Palm Desktop by choosing Save Archive Copy on PC.

Working with Notes

The Note Pad is similar to the Memo Pad. The major difference is this: instead of writing long messages in Graffiti, you're sketching or writing them directly on the screen, as if the stylus were a pen writing on paper. Though Note Pad gives you the freedom to write anything on the screen any way you like, keep in mind that you can't transform this "digital ink" into Graffiti. Your scribbles stay scribbles. When Note Pad starts, you'll see the Note List view (which looks a lot like the Memo Pad's Memo List view).

Creating a Note

To create a note, tap the New button at the bottom of the screen (you can also just start writing in the Graffiti area). Start your note by giving it a name. Unlike memos, all notes get their own unique subject line. By default, this subject begins with a "time stamp," though you can erase that if you want to.

When you're ready to draw, just write or sketch in the main part of the Zire's display. Here are the controls at your disposal:

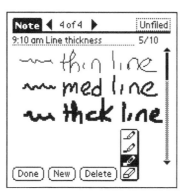

Alarming a Note

Unlike those yellow sticky notes you leave all over your office walls (clean up already—it looks like a pig sty!), the notes you leave in your Zire can actually buzz you at a certain time and date. Why on earth would you want that to happen, you ask? The following is a good example.

You're stopped at a red light when you hear on the car radio that Diana Darby is playing a show in town in a few weeks. You'd love to go to the concert, so you whip out your Zire. The light will turn green in a moment, though, so you don't have a lot of time to write. Instead of trying your luck with Graffiti, you simply press the Note Pad button and scrawl "Diana Darby" on the screen. Then you quickly choose Options | Alarm from the menu and choose Saturday at 10 A.M., which is when the tickets go on sale. Tap OK, and when Saturday morning rolls around, the Zire will turn on, bring your note to the front, and play the alarm. As you probably expect, you can accept the alarm or tap the Snooze button:

Working in the Palm Desktop

You can create and review your notes and memos on the Palm Desktop. That's good, because many kinds of memos might come in handy on the desktop. If you took our advice from earlier in the chapter to create a Phone Messages memo, for instance, you'd appreciate the capability to type directly into the PC when the phone rings.

Because the Zire has pretty limited real estate on the small screen, you have to switch between the Memo List and Memo view, but on the Palm Desktop, you can see both at once. To see a memo, click the header on the left, and the memo's contents appear in the window on the right (see Figure 8-2). Double-clicking a memo header has no effect.

Most of the Memo Pad's operation is obvious. The controls aren't identical, though. Here are some things to remember:

- You can't rearrange memos; you can sort them alphabetically or by the way they appear on the Zire. Use the Sort By drop-down menu at the top of the screen.

- You can display memos in a list or by icons (like Outlook's Notes) using the tabs at the bottom of the screen.

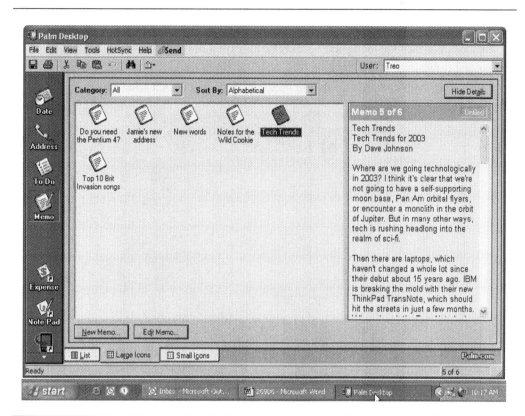

FIGURE 8-2   The Palm Desktop has a convenient text window for viewing your notes.

Importing and Exporting Memos

You don't need to create memos from scratch. Heck, you don't even have to cut and paste to create a memo. The Palm Desktop lets you import text files from elsewhere on the computer. To import a text file, do this:

1. Choose File | Import. The Import dialog box appears.

2. Choose Text (*.txt) from the File of Type list box.

3. Find the file you want to import. It has to be a plaintext file in ASCII format—no Word or other specially formatted file types are allowed. Select the file and click the Open button. You then see the Specify Import Fields dialog box.

4. The text file should be ready to import, with the text lined up with the Memo field. If it isn't, drag the Memo field on the left until it lines up like the one shown here:

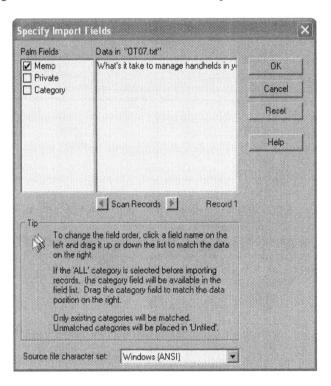

5. Click OK.

6. If your text file is too large to fit in a single memo, the Palm Desktop automatically divides it into multiple memos.

7. Click OK.

What about the other case—you have a memo and you'd like to get it into Microsoft Word? Piece of cake! Just right-click on a memo and choose Send To | MS Word from the menu. The text will automatically appear in a new blank document in Word.

NOTE
For the Send To feature to work, you need to have the Palmapp.dot template installed in Microsoft Word. Some folks delete that template and then are mystified why they can't send documents to Word. On the other hand, you can always get text into Word the old-fashioned way: copy and paste.

The Windows Note Pad

The Note Pad is a little more limited. You can't create notes on the desktop, for instance; all you can do is look at ones you created on your Zire. Notes won't alarm on the desktop, either, so if you want to be alerted when a note's time comes up, you'll have to have your Zire with you.

Besides looking at notes, you can also export them to a graphics program. Don't expect to stick one of these sketches into a high-resolution PowerPoint presentation, of course. A Note Pad image measures just 152×352 pixels, which is not enough to fill a computer screen, but getting your handiwork into a graphics program is easy. Just do this:

1. Press the Note Pad button on the left side of the Palm Desktop display. You should see the Note Pad window appear.

2. Find the note in the list that you want to export.

3. Right-click on the note (either in the List view or on the image itself) and choose Copy from the menu.

4. Open your favorite image editing program and choose Edit | Paste from the menu.

8

Look Ma, No Scroll Bar!

Outlook's notes have an annoying glitch—lacking scroll bars, it's hard to read a long note that trails off the bottom of the sticky note window. Don't know what we're talking about? Copy a long Word document into a new note, or create a really long memo and HotSync. You'll find the that text extends beyond the bottom of the note window in Outlook and there's no scroll bar to scroll down to read it all.

The solution is deceptively simple: click in the note window to place the cursor in the note and then use the down arrow key on the keyboard to scroll through the document, or make the note's window larger so it can show more text.

Why do we mention this? Rick didn't realize there was any way to scroll through the document at all—he thought anything that didn't fit in the sticky note window was totally inaccessible—until Dave showed him the keyboard arrow trick. So, if you were ever perplexed by the missing memo text, now you are at least as smart as Rick (fill in your own jokes here).

Using Outlook with the Zire

Outlook's Notes view is, like the Zire's Memo Pad, a place to store free-form notes of any kind. You can use it to record phone messages, jot down reminders, leave long-term documents (like things to bring on a trip), or to remind yourself about Web sites you want to visit. It doesn't matter what you put in these notes. By default, Outlook's notes look like little Post-it notes. You can change their appearance in two ways:

1. To change the color of a single note, right-click it and choose Color from the menu. You can choose from five colors to make certain notes stand out visually.

2. To change the default color and size of all notes, choose Tools | Options from the Outlook menu and click the Preferences tab. Click the Note Options button and set your preferences. Click OK to close the dialog boxes. All new notes you create appear with these settings.

Quirks Between Outlook and Zire

While the Outlook Notes view and Palm Memo Pad are perhaps the simplest of all the features in these two programs, there are a few things you should know to ensure everything works smoothly when you HotSync:

1. The Palm Memo Pad has a size limit—but Notes in Outlook don't. This means you can create a very long note in Outlook that doesn't transfer properly to the Zire. If you create a huge note in Outlook, only the first 4,096 characters appear in the Memo Pad. You also see a warning in the HotSync log saying this occurred.

2. The Zire's categories aren't used by Outlook. This means your memos, when they appear in Outlook as notes, are unfiled. The same is true in the other direction.

A Memo Pad Alternative

Is the Memo Pad not powerful enough for you? Then flip over to Chapter 11, where we introduce you to a few powerful word-processing alternatives to the Memo Pad, such as Documents To Go and WordSmith. There's also a program called Memo PLUS, which enables you to attach drawings to your memos, use templates, and more. Memo PLUS is a good program you might choose to use instead of the Memo Pad. Find it on the Web at **www.handshigh.com**.

Where to Find It

Web Site	Address	What's There
SmartCell Technology	**www.smartcell.com**	TextPlus
High Hands Software	**www.handshigh.com**	Memo PLUS
PalmGear	**www.palmgear.com**	Tons of additional software

8

Chapter 9

The Rest of the Palm OS Team

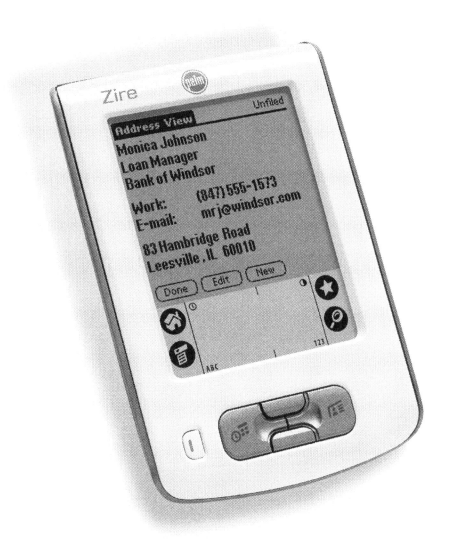

How to...

- Access security features
- Set records as private
- Hide or show private records
- Set a security password
- Password-protect your Zire
- Find third-party security measures for your Zire and data
- Use the Find feature
- Use the calculator
- Find third-party calculators
- Use a Zire to track expenses and mileage
- Make effective use of categories
- Synchronize your expenses with Excel
- Synchronize your expenses on a Macintosh
- Find other expense-management software and solutions

Now that we've looked at the stars of the Palm OS—the Address Book, Date Book, Memo Pad, and To Do List—let's turn our attention to the supporting cast. We're talking about the Security program, which enables you to hide private records and "lock" your Zire; the Find feature, a search tool that helps you quickly sift through all your data; the calculator, which (big surprise) calculates; and the often-ignored Expense program.

Zire Security

At the risk of sounding like a spy novel, listen up, 007. If your data falls into the wrong hands, it could spell disaster for *M, Q,* and lots of other letters of the alphabet. Fortunately, we've outfitted your Zire with foolproof security measures. Only you will have the access codes. Only you can view Heather Graham's phone number. (Can we have it? Please? Please?)

In all seriousness, it's not unlikely that you'll be storing some sensitive information in your Zire, information that should be kept private. Important passwords, account numbers, meeting locations, contact data—these are among the items you'd be loathe to let a stranger see. Fortunately, the Palm OS offers two effective ways to protect your data: marking individual records as private, and locking your Zire every time you turn it off.

In both scenarios, you—or anyone who's trying to access your Zire—must supply a password to gain access. It's a bit of a hassle to have to enter it over and over again, but at least you have the comfort of knowing your Zire and data are totally secure.

Security 101

To get started with Zire security, find and tap the Security icon. You'll see the screen shown in Figure 9-1. The first step is choosing a password. Notice that the Password box currently says Unassigned—meaning simply that you haven't entered your password yet. Before you do, read a little further.

 Capitalization doesn't matter. Even if you make a point to capitalize "Spock" when you enter it as your new password, you can write "spock" to unlock your Zire, and it'll work just fine.

What You Should Know About Passwords

The password you choose can be any combination of letters, numbers, symbols, and spaces. You can make it "Spock" or "H4T*Q" or "The quick brown fox." Ideally, it should be something reasonably short, as you'll probably wind up writing it frequently. Don't make it too obvious, like "123," but you could use something as simple as the last four digits of your Social Security number or your mother's maiden name.

 *Whatever password you decide on, it's vital that it be something you can easily remember. If you forget it, you could wind up unable to access certain records—or your entire Zire! Thus, if you have even the slightest concern that you might forget your password, write it down on a piece of paper and store it in a safe place. Better safe than sorry.*

9

Working with Passwords

Okay, let's enter a new password on your Zire. Just tap the Unassigned box and then use Graffiti or the onscreen keyboard to enter your desired password.

FIGURE 9-1   In Security, you select a password for use in hiding private records and locking your Zire.

 *At this time you're also asked to supply a hint. If you use, say, your mother's maiden name as your password, you should put "mother's maiden name" in the hint field. This hint appears when an incorrect password is entered.*

Note the warning that's included here: "If you assign a password, you must enter it to show private records." This sounds a little scary, but don't worry—none of your existing records will immediately be affected by your selection of a password. Only when you mark one as private, as we explain later, does your password enter into play.

After you tap OK, you'll be asked to verify the new password by entering it again. Then you'll see another warning about what'll happen if your password is forgotten. The moral of the story is, *don't forget your password!*

Tap OK again, and notice that the Password box now reads Assigned.

TIP *You can tap this box again at any time to change or delete your password, but you have to supply the original one first.*

Now, when you mark records as private, they become hidden from view, requiring your password to reveal them. Additionally, if you use the Lock & Turn Off option (as detailed in the following section), you'll need to supply your password the next time you turn on your Zire.

SHORTCUT *If you tap the "abc" button in the lower-left corner of the Graffiti area, the onscreen keyboard will appear. You can use this to enter your password!*

Password-Protecting Your Entire Handheld

If you really want to secure what's stored in your Zire, you need to password-protect the entire thing, not just certain records. That's where "locking" comes into play. When activated, your Zire becomes locked the next time it's turned off. Translation: When the Zire is turned on again, a screen pops up requiring the password (see Figure 9-2). Without it, there's no getting past that screen.

 *You can modify the information that appears on this "locked" startup screen by going to Prefs | Owner (see Chapter 2 for a refresher). We recommend including your name and phone number, and maybe even a reward offer—all so that anyone who might find your lost Zire will have an easier time returning it (and an incentive to do so). What's a good reward? Considering how much a new Zire would cost you, we think no less than $20.*

The "Lost Password" Button

Oh, the perils of the forgotten password. For the last time, just don't forget yours, okay? If you do, there's a scary but effective way to reestablish access to those records you've marked as private. In Security, when you tap the Assigned button under Password, you're prompted to enter your password. You also see a "Lost Password" button. Tap it, and your password will be deleted—and all your marked-as-private records along with it. However, those deleted records will be restored on your Zire the next time you HotSync.

FIGURE 9-2   When you "lock" your Zire, only the correct password will unlock it.

Auto Lock Handheld   The Palm OS includes several automated locking options, all of them accessible by tapping the Auto Lock Handheld button in the main Security screen. Here's a quick rundown:

- **Never**   No automatic locking.
- **On power off**   The moment you turn your handheld off (or it shuts off after a few minutes of inactivity), it locks.
- **At a preset time**   Set the handheld to lock at an exact time. For example, if you use it a lot during the day, but rarely at night, you might set it to lock at, say, 6:00 P.M. That way, you won't have to keep entering your password all day.
- **After a preset delay**   This is our favorite option. It locks the handheld after a period of inactivity—ten minutes, three hours, whatever you choose.

The "Current Privacy" Menu

We've saved the Current Privacy option till last because it relates to the upcoming section on hiding and masking individual records. Simply put, when the Hide option is selected, all records you've marked as private will disappear from view. When you select Mask, private records are hidden but still listed. When you select Show, which you need your password to do, private records are made visible.

9

Hiding and Masking Your Records

In the four main applications—Address Book, Date Book, Memo Pad, and To Do List—any record can be marked private, meaning it suddenly becomes masked or invisible and, therefore, inaccessible. Here's how:

1. Select a record (just by tapping it) in any of the aforementioned programs.

2. Tap the Details button. (In Address Book, you have to tap Edit to get to the screen with the Details button.) You'll see a window containing some options for that record—and a box labeled Private.

3. Tap that box, noticing the check mark that appears. This indicates that the record will become private after you tap OK.

4. Tap OK.

Remember, marking a record as private has no effect unless you've chosen one of the two privacy options in the Security program. If it's set to Mask Records, records you've marked as private will turn into a solid gray bars. If you choose Hide Records, records will just plain disappear. (Don't freak out—they're still in memory, just not visible.)

The Difference Between Masking and Hiding

The Mask Records option provides a middle ground between the visibility of "shown" records and the total invisibility of "hidden" records (which appear to have been wiped from existence—great security, but awfully inconvenient). Masked records still appear in your phone list, memo pad, and so forth but appear as solid gray bars (see Figure 9-3). This remains a less-than-stellar solution, as there's still no way to know what lies beneath until you tap the record and enter your password.

FIGURE 9-3 When you choose Mask Records, all records marked as private are hidden by gray bars.

The Hide Records option goes a major step further, removing marked-as-private records from view altogether. To make them visible again, you must return to Security and select Show Records. Naturally, you'll need to supply your password at this time.

Passwords on the Desktop

Security isn't limited to the Zire itself. It also extends to Palm Desktop, working in much the same ways. Thus, you can hide certain records or password-protect the entire program. The same password you've selected for your Zire will automatically be used in Desktop.

Unfortunately, this is an area in which Mac users get the short shrift. Palm Desktop for Macintosh doesn't include any security features whatsoever. While you can still keep your data protected on your Zire, anyone who has access to your computer has access to your info (unless you've installed some third-party security software).

Only Palm Desktop is affected by masked and hidden records. If you synchronize with Microsoft Outlook or another third-party contact manager, records marked as private on your Zire will still be visible on your PC.

Hidden Records

Whenever you HotSync, any records marked as private on your Zire will become hidden in Palm Desktop—and vice versa. To change whether private records are visible or not, click the View menu and select the desired option: Hide, Mask, or Show.

Password-Protecting Palm Desktop

Just as you can lock your Zire, so can you lock Palm Desktop. When you do this and exit the program, your password will be required the next time it's started—by you or anyone else. Here's how to activate this setting:

1. Make sure Palm Desktop is running and click Tools | Options.

2. In the tabbed dialog box that appears, click the Security tab.

3. Click the box that says "Require password to access the Palm Desktop data."

4. Click OK and exit Palm Desktop.

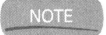
This security setting applies only to your data. If multiple users are sharing Palm Desktop on a single PC, they'll need to implement password protection for their own user profiles.

Other Security Software

While the Palm Operating System's built-in security features are fairly comprehensive, there's always room for improvement. Hence the availability of numerous third-party security programs, which generally offer greater versatility and/or convenience. Here we spotlight some of the more intriguing solutions.

MobileSafe

Your Zire can be a handy place to store account numbers, PIN numbers, passwords, and other secret codes, but stuffing them all into a memo isn't the most practical solution. HandMark's MobileSafe, one of Rick's personal favorites, is designed expressly to organize and protect your important numbers and passwords. You need to remember only one password (different from the one used by Zire Security) to access all this neatly categorized information. MobileSafe also has a Windows-based counterpart, so you can manage and access the information on your PC.

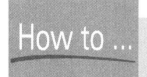 **Keep Others from Accessing Palm Desktop**

Suppose you step away from your desk for lunch or a meeting. You don't want coworkers or corporate spies poking around through your records. Fortunately, there's an easy way to password-protect Palm Desktop for Windows (alas, the Macintosh version has no security features). Choose Tools | Options, click the Security tab, and check the box marked "Require password to access the Palm Desktop data." Now, whenever someone starts Palm Desktop, they must input the correct password (which is the one you created on your handheld) to access their data.

 While Rick is a fan of MobileSafe, Dave likes Chapura's Cloak—a similar product. It's worth checking out if you're interested in this kind of security.

OnlyMe

Like Security on steroids, OnlyMe locks your Zire automatically whenever it's turned off. Your password is entered by tapping on a special six-button keypad, pressing the Zire's buttons in a particular sequence, or entering certain letters or numbers in the Graffiti area. You can even create a password that's based on sliding your stylus over the special keypad. Best of all, OnlyMe lets you set a "lock delay," so that your Zire won't lock until after a designated period of time has elapsed.

Sign-On

Passwords can be guessed or discovered, but it's a lot harder to duplicate your signature. Communication Intelligence Corp.'s Sign-On automatically locks your Zire when it's turned off and then requires you to sign your name—right on the Zire's screen—to unlock it again. This is a great choice for those concerned about forgetting their password.

The Find Feature

The more you use your Zire, the more data you're likely to wind up storing, and the more data you have, the harder it can be to expediently find what you're looking for. Some examples:

- A couple of days ago, you set up a meeting a few weeks in the future, and now you want to check the details of that meeting. Must you page through your calendar a day at a time to find the entry?

- You've got dozens of memos and need to find the ones containing the word "sponge." Must you open each memo individually?

- You have 1,500 names in your address list and want to quickly find the record for that guy named Apu whose last name and company you can't remember. How will you locate him?

Using the Palm Operating System's built-in Find feature, you can unearth all this information in a snap. True to its name, Find sifts through your databases to ferret out exactly what you're looking for, be it a name, a number, a word, a phrase, or even just a few letters.

As we showed you in Chapter 2, Find can be found in the lower-right corner of the Graffiti area, represented by a little magnifying-glass icon. Using it couldn't be simpler: Tap it (at any time, no matter what program you're running) and then write in what you want to search for (see Figure 9-4).

 *Capitalization doesn't matter. Even if you're looking for a proper name like "Caroline," you needn't capitalize the first letter.*

The search process should take no more than a few seconds, depending on how many records you've got on your Zire and the complexity of your search criteria.

 *If you use your stylus to highlight a word or chunk of text (done much the same way you select text using a mouse), that text will automatically appear in the Find field when you tap the Find icon.*

How Find Works

When you execute a search, the Palm OS looks through all stored records (except those marked as private) for whatever text you've specified, starting with whatever program you were in when you tapped the Find icon. It looks not only in the main databases—those used by Address Book, Memo Pad, and so forth—but also in the databases associated with any third-party software you may have installed.

 *If you're looking for, say, a phone number, you can save a lot of time by loading the Address Book before tapping Find. That's because Find starts its search in whatever program is currently running.*

FIGURE 9-4   Looking for a specific word? Just write it in the Find box, and the Zire will find it for you.

Keep in mind that Find searches only the beginnings of words. Thus, if you look up "book," it will find "bookcase" but not "handbook." There are third-party programs that can perform much more thorough searches—we talk about some of them in the next section.

You can make your data a bit more "Find friendly" by using special modifiers. For instance, you might use the letters AP *to preface any memo that has to do with Accounts Payable. Then, when you do a search for "AP," you'll quickly unearth all the relevant records.*

Running a Search

After you've written the desired search text in the Find box and tapped OK, the Zire will get to work. You'll see items appear in a categorized list as they're found. If you see what you're looking for, you can halt the search immediately by tapping the Stop button. Then, simply tap the item to bring up the corresponding record in the corresponding program.

If the Zire finds more instances of the desired item than can fit on the screen at once, it will stop the search until you tap the Find More button. This essentially tells it to look up another screen's worth of records. There's no way to backtrack—to return to the previous screen—so make sure you need to keep searching before tapping Find More. (You can always run the search again if need be, but that's a hassle.)

Third-Party Search Programs

Many users find that Find isn't nearly as robust as it could be. If you want to maximize the search potential of your Zire, one the following third-party programs might be in order. They're a little on the advanced side, meaning they require the program HackMaster. That doesn't mean you should shy away from them, just that they might prove a little more complicated to install and operate.

FIGURE 9-5   The Zire calculator functions like every other calculator you've ever used.

The Calculator

What's an electronic organizer without a calculator? Not much, so let's take a quick peek at the Zire's. Activated by tapping the Calc icon, Calculator operates like any other, well, calculator (see Figure 9-5). In fact, it's so self-explanatory that we're not going to insult your intelligence by explaining how to use it.

There are, of course, one or two features we feel obligated to point out. First, you can use the standard Palm OS copy option to paste the result of any calculation into another program. Second, you can review your last few calculations by tapping Menu | Options | Recent Calculations.

 *Calc's buttons are large enough that you can tap them with a fingernail, so save time by leaving the stylus in its silo. Just keep in mind that oil and dirt from your fingers will grubby-up the screen.*

Third-Party Calculators

Whether you're a student, realtor, banker, or NASA engineer, there's no debating the value of a good scientific and/or programmable calculator. Your Zire has ample processing power to fill this role, and the proof is in the dozens of third-party calculators currently available. Let's take a look at some of the best and brightest.

FCPlus Professional and the powerOne Series

Aimed at financial, real estate, and retail professionals, Infinity Softworks' FCPlus Professional is one of the most sophisticated calculators around. It offers more than 400 built-in business, math, finance, and statistics functions and includes memory worksheets for keeping track of various computations. If anything, FCPlus Professional might be overkill, but if you need this kind of power, you'll love the program.

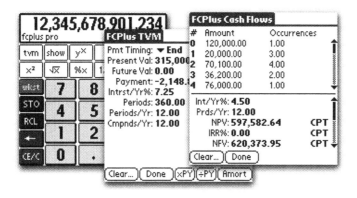

Infinity Softworks also offers a series of task-specific calculators: powerOne Finance, powerOne Graph, and powerOne Scientific.

SynCalc

A fully algebraic calculator, Synergy Solutions' SynCalc offers a unique plug-in architecture that allows new functionality to be added. As it stands, SynCalc is already plenty powerful, with algebraic parsing of expressions, a full suite of trigonometric and logarithmic functions, and support for up to 100 macros that simplify the execution of complex calculations.

All About Expense

Expense is an often-overlooked but decidedly valuable addition to the Zire software arsenal. With it, you can track and manage all your expenses and mileage, whether for personal reconciliation or reimbursement from your company or clients. While a bit on the rudimentary side, Expense does afford quick and easy item entry and direct synchronization with Palm Desktop. It can also export items to Microsoft Excel, creating detailed and attractive-looking expense reports that are ready to print.

Getting Started with Expense

Put simply, Expense is like an electronic folder for your receipts and a logbook for your mileage. Whenever you buy something, you simply add it to your expense list. Whenever you take a business-related road trip, you do the same. On the Zire side, using Expense is a piece of cake. Using it with Palm Desktop is just as easy, but we'll talk about that a little later.

Creating New Expense Items

Adding new expense records is a snap. Here's the basic process:

1. Tap New to create a blank expense item. You see a line appear with the date, the words "-Expense type-", and a blank field next to a dollar sign. Note that your cursor appears in that field.

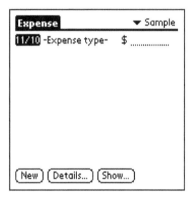

2. Write in the amount of the purchase or, if you're recording mileage, the number of miles driven.

3. Now, tap the words "-Expense type-" to see a predefined list of expense categories, and choose the one that most closely matches your purchase. If you're recording mileage, select that option, noticing that the dollar sign changes to the abbreviation "mi."

 *Unlike most lists that appear in Zire applications, the Expense list cannot be modified or expanded. In short, you're stuck with the categories provided. If you can't find one that fits the situation, there's always the Other category.*

4. By default, any new expense is created with the current date. If, however, you're catching up on previous purchases, you can tap right on the date that's shown to bring up the calendar and select whatever date is appropriate.

There, wasn't that easy? You've just recorded a new expense. Now let's talk about recording the more specific details of that expense.

 You can save yourself a step when you create a new expense by not tapping the New button first. Instead, just start writing the dollar amount in the numeric portion of the Graffiti area. A new expense item is instantly created. This same practice also works in Date Book, Memo Pad, and To Do List.

Modifying Expense Details

Obviously, any expense report worth its salt needs to have more than just the date, expense type, and amount. As you probably guessed, your next stop after entering these tidbits is the Details button.

 Before tapping it, make sure you select the expense item you want to modify. You know when an item is selected because the date is highlighted and a cursor appears in the Amount field.

The Receipt Details screen (see Figure 9–6) lets you specify the minutiae of your purchase, from the category to which it belongs to the type of currency used to the city in which it took place.

9

FIGURE 9-6   You can record any or all of the crucial details of your expense in the Receipt Details screen.

Expense in Palm Desktop

As with the other core Zire applications (Address Book, Memo Pad, and so on), Expense synchronizes its data with Palm Desktop every time you HotSync. Likewise, any additions or changes you make in Palm Desktop are reflected on your Zire.

As you can see in Figure 9-7, Palm Desktop keeps your Expense entries in a neat list. If you click the tabs at the bottom of the screen, you can view the items as icons (large or small), which can help you get an at-a-glance overview of the kinds of expenses you've incurred. If you need a hard copy, just choose Print from the File menu. You can choose to print an expense summary, a list of expense details, or both.

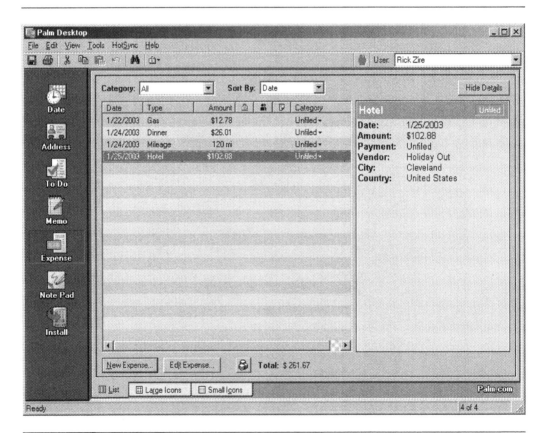

FIGURE 9-7   Palm Desktop displays and organizes your Expense data, just as it does with your addresses, appointments, and so on.

From Expense to Excel

You can also export your Expense data to Microsoft Word or Excel, provided you have those programs installed on your PC. This can be helpful if you need to include your Expense data in a preformatted invoice or spreadsheet. To start the process, click Edit | Send To and choose Word or Excel from the list that appears. That's all there is to it!

Alternatives to Expense

Truth be told, Expense isn't the most robust expense-management program—especially relative to some of the software created by third-party developers. If your needs extend beyond what Expense has to offer—and for businesspeople who rely heavily on reimbursement reports, they probably do—you should definitely check out one of the many available alternatives.

We've spotlighted some of the major programs, but keep in mind that these are designed for expense tracking only. There are other programs that manage billing, as well as expenses, and that let you track your bank accounts and stock portfolios. (We talk about those in Chapter 16.) So don't be discouraged if none of these packages fit your particular bill. Chances are good there's a program out there that will.

ExpenseDirector

Iambic Software's *ExpenseDirector* lets you track expenses by type, account, payee, client, project, and the currency for the expense. It supports the creation of customized item lists, so your data entry speeds up over time. Particularly noteworthy are the program's filtering and sorting options, which let you view records for a single day or a range of days and sort by any of the aforementioned tracking criteria.

```
┌────────────────────────────────────┐
│ Expense Entry        │Fri 3/6/01│   │
│ Amount: 37.50          ▼ $US        │
│   Detail: Dave Jaynes               │
│   ─────────────────────────────     │
│ Payee: Muleto's               ▼     │
│  Type: ▼ Meals                      │
│  Trip: ▼ None                       │
│ Account: ▼ VISA                     │
│ Project: ▼ Amcom:Web Design         │
│   ☑ Receipt     ☐ Reported          │
│   ☑ Billable    ☐ Private           │
│  (Done) (Notes) (Delete)            │
└────────────────────────────────────┘
```

One hitch: ExpenseDirector can synchronize data to your Windows PC, but only with Iambic's ExpenseDirector for Windows—a separate program that's equally robust on the PC side. You can buy ExpenseDirector alone for $29.95 or bundled with its Windows counterpart for $59.95.

ExpensePlus

One of the most robust and versatile expense managers available, WalletWare's *ExpensePlus* uses an icon-based interface to simplify the selection of expense types and automation to fill in dates and amounts for things like hotel stays and car rentals. More important, it can link directly to any existing company expense forms created in Excel or FileMaker (including the Mac versions), so you needn't contend with nonstandard forms. Also, if your company's forms aren't based in Excel, WalletWare can design a custom link (for a fee) to other software programs.

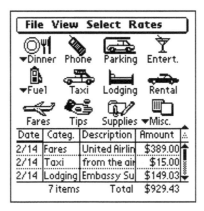

Where to Find It

Web Site	Address	What's There
Handmark	www.handmark.com	MobileSafe
Chapura	www.chapura.com	Cloak
Tranzoa	www.tranzoa.com	OnlyMe
CIC	www.cic.com	Sign-On
Infinity Softworks	www.infinitysw.com	FC Plus Professional, powerOne series
Synergy Solutions	www.synsolutions.com	SynCalc
Iambic Software	www.iambic.com	ExpenseDirector
WalletWare	www.walletware.com	ExpensePlus

Chapter 10

The Internet in Your Zire

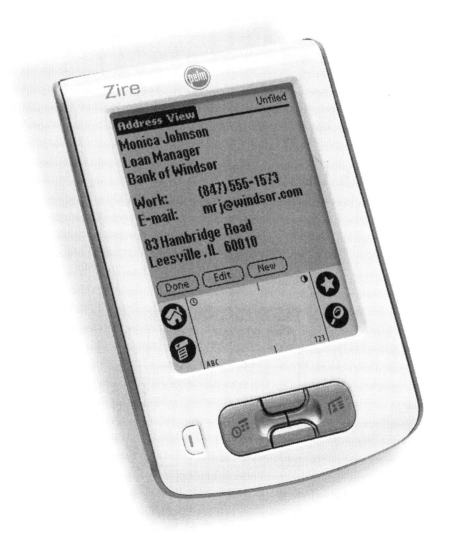

How to...

- Use AvantGo to take the Web with you
- Download and install AvantGo
- Configure AvantGo's Web "channels"
- Use AvantGo to download MapQuest directions to your Zire
- Use AvantGo to keep local movie listings on your Zire
- Download local hot-spot info with Vindigo

Of all the cool things your Zire can do, Web browsing is definitely one of the coolest. You're probably thinking, "Uh, oh, here we go, now I need to buy an expensive, complicated modem or something, right?" Wrong! Part of what makes this so cool is that your Zire can access the Web *without* a modem. Well, sort of.

In this chapter, we introduce you to several terrific third-party programs: AvantGo, HandStory, and Vindigo. These programs enable your Zire to access the Web—but, again, not in the traditional sense. Instead, your Zire takes advantage of your computer's modem to download data during the HotSync process. We'll explain in greater detail in the sections to come.

Channel Surf with AvantGo

Lots of modern mobile phones and handheld PCs boast Web-browsing features, but let's be real—the Web just doesn't fit on a 2-inch screen. Enter AvantGo, a free service that not only delivers Web-based content to your Zire, but also formats it to look pretty (and readable). With every HotSync, the software downloads your preselected channels—everything from news and stock reports to driving directions and movie show times—using your computer's modem to ferry the data. Pretty slick—and did we mention it's free?

 *At press time, AvantGo had just been purchased by another company. While we certainly hope the service will continue running, the new owners might choose to shut it down—or start charging for it.*

Just What Is a "Third-Party Program," Anyway?

In this chapter and the chapters to come, we talk a lot about "third-party programs." This refers to software developed by companies (and, in some cases, individuals) other than Palm. Why do we make this distinction? Simply to help differentiate between the software that comes in the box and software you obtain elsewhere. All the programs mentioned in this chapter were developed not by Palm, but by other companies.

Set Up AvantGo

To install the AvantGo software, visit the AvantGo Web site and download the software. Install it as per the directions in the package and configure your AvantGo account. You'll need to set up an AvantGo account, complete with username and password.

To set up the channels you want to transfer to your Zire, go to the AvantGo Web site and log in. The AvantGo site should look something like the one shown in Figure 10-1, in which your currently selected channels appear in a tabbed box called My Device. You can browse the AvantGo Web site and click on any channel you like to add it to your personal AvantGo hot list.

Make Changes to Channels

Each channel has its own settings: size (meaning how much memory it consumes), image inclusion (whether or not graphics are included with the channel), refresh rate (how often updates are downloaded to your Zire), and so on. You can modify these settings by clicking any channel shown in your My Device list.

The one you may want to consider modifying right away is Channel Refresh (see Figure 10-2). By default, each channel is "refreshed" (meaning its content is downloaded) each and every time you HotSync. Ah, but the HotSync process tends to take a lot longer with AvantGo installed, especially if you have a lot of channels. Also, if you HotSync more than once per day, you

10

The Single Best Reason to Use AvantGo

Most computer users are familiar with MapQuest, the Web site that generates door-to-door driving directions. If you have AvantGo installed on your Zire, you can turn any given set of directions into an AvantGo channel with just a few mouse clicks. Here's how: visit the MapQuest site and use it like you normally would to get directions. Once the route is displayed, find and click the button marked "Download to Your PDA." From there you're taken to a screen where you can name your route. Then click Save Route and follow the subsequent instructions. On your next HotSync, the route will be transferred to your Zire, where you can view it in AvantGo like any other channel. Now that's cool.

FIGURE 10-1   AvantGo lets you transfer Web "channels" to your Zire for offline reading.

Our AvantGo Favorites

Dave: The Zire's Address Book and Date Book are fine, but I'd be lost without AvantGo. Whenever I go out for lunch alone (and that happens a lot more than I'd like), sit around in the airport, or have nothing better to do, I whip out my PDA and read the latest AvantGo channels. My favorites are the Joke A Day page, the New York Times, and The Onion. I also remain an up-to-date geek by reading the SciFi Channel, CNET News, and Palm Infocenter, but as you'll see by Rick's choices (which no doubt include Knitting Today, Barbie Collectors Daily, and the Zima "Clearly Refreshing Beverage" Newsletter), there's something on AvantGo for everyone.

Rick: As usual, all of Dave's claims are false—except for the part about being a geek. Here's a guy whose DVD collection includes the cheesy 1970s TV show *UFO*. Anyway, my preferred AvantGo channels include CNN, Hollywood.com, and SciFi Channel (yes, I'm a geek, too, but not even remotely in Dave's league). I also like to download MapQuest driving directions (see "The Single Best Reason to Use AvantGo"). Now, if you'll excuse me, I have to get back to my knitting.

probably don't want to wait several minutes for the process to complete. Thus, we recommend changing each channel's setting from On Every Sync to Once Daily. That way, you'll still get new content every day, but subsequent HotSyncs won't take nearly as long.

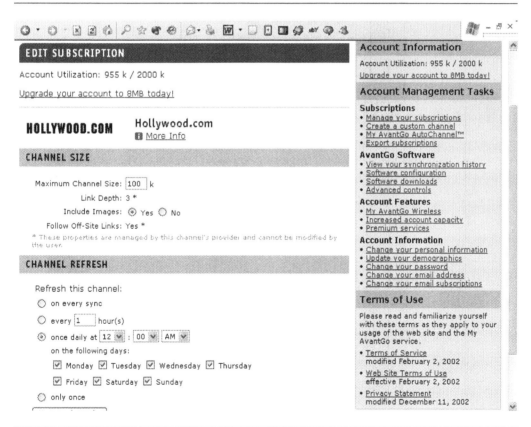

FIGURE 10-2   You can modify the amount of data contained in each channel from this page.

10

Use AvantGo on Your Zire

Using AvantGo is not unlike using a Web browser on your PC. There's a "back" button that returns you to the previous page, and underlined "hotlinks" you tap to load additional pages. Let's take AvantGo for a spin. When you tap the AvantGo icon, you should see the list of channels you selected and configured on the Web.

NOTE *If you don't see any channels in AvantGo, it's probably because you haven't HotSynced yet. Remember, that's how channels get from your PC to your Zire.*

To use AvantGo, just tap one of the channels in the My Channels list. You can read text, view pictures, and drill deeper into the channel by tapping on links. There are two navigational tools built into each and every channel page:

- Tap the navigational arrows to move forward and backward through the current channel.
- Tap the Home icon to return to the My Channels list.

The Second Best Reason to Use AvantGo

How often has this happened to you? You're in a restaurant having dinner and decide you'd like to take in a movie afterward. Problem is you don't have a newspaper handy, so you don't know what's playing where. Enter Hollywood.com, one of the all-time great AvantGo channels. After you add it to your channel list and HotSync your Zire, open the channel on your Zire. You'll see a field where you can enter your ZIP code. Once that's done (it's a one-time task), HotSync again. The next time you open the Hollywood.com channel on your Zire, you'll find complete, up-to-date movie listings for your area! And they'll get updated again every time you HotSync. Ain't technology grand?

Vindigo: A Concierge in Your Pocket

Imagine a service like AvantGo that's devoted entirely to local entertainment and information. That's Vindigo in a nutshell. It delivers an abundance of city-specific listings to your handheld: restaurants, museums, shops, stores, movie theaters, and so on, as well as practical information like locations of police stations, hospitals, ATMs, and more. It can even show you maps of specific locations. In short, it's like having a concierge in your pocket, one that knows your city inside and out.

Vindigo is available for more than 50 cities across the U.S., so check the Web site to see if yours is represented. The real concern is memory: listings for any given city can be as large as 1MB—half your Zire's total memory. However, you can lower Vindigo's consumption by selecting only those listings you really want (that is, you don't have to download everything— you can custom-tailor Vindigo to provide only the content you want).

Vindigo costs $24.95 for a one-year subscription or $3.50 per month. Fortunately, as with most Palm OS products, you can try before you buy. The service offers a free trial so you can see if you like the service. We think you will.

Where to Find It

Web Site	Address	What's There
AvantGo	**www.avantgo.com**	AvantGo
Vindigo	**www.vindigo.com**	Vindigo

Chapter 11

Throw Away Your PC!

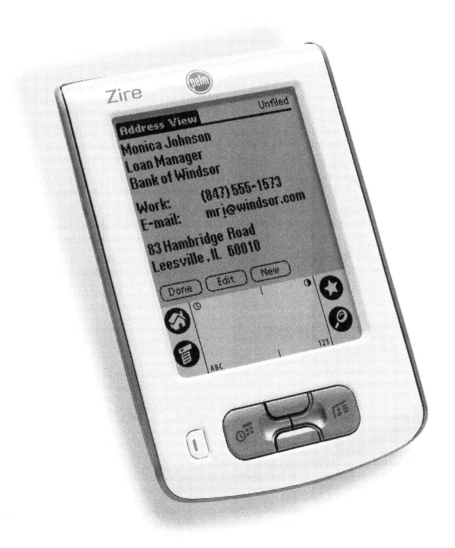

How to...

- Use your Zire as a handheld laptop computer
- Read and edit Word and Excel documents on your Zire
- Tell the difference between Zire's doc and Word's .doc files
- Import Zire documents into Microsoft Word
- Generate graphs and charts on the Zire
- View Adobe Acrobat files
- Project PowerPoint slides via your Zire
- Print from your PDA

The core applications that come with your Zire are fine for many people—they offer all the basic tools you need to stay on top of your key contact information and schedule while on the go, but, as you've already seen, your Zire can do so much more. In fact, it's almost possible to use your Zire as a sort of miniature laptop, capable of running apps like a word processor and spreadsheet.

Why on earth would you want to do that? Well, which would you rather carry around—a Zire that slips in your pocket or a seven-pound laptop? Which is easier to store in a hotel room? Which is more likely to get stolen? Which lasts longer on a set of batteries? We think you get the idea. Obviously, using a suite of "office" applications on your Zire isn't for everyone and won't work all the time. After all, your Zire has a limited amount of storage space, so you can't fit a whole lot of documents on it. Most Zire document editors don't support an extensive array of formatting options, either, so even if you exchange documents with your desktop apps, your text and format options may be somewhat limited, but if you're intrigued by the thought of leaving your PC at home and traveling only with a Zire, then read on. This chapter is all about creating the perfect handheld office.

Building the Perfect Beast

The name of the game when it comes to creating an office suite for your Zire is convenience and compatibility. What good is it, for instance, to generate documents on your PDA if they're not readable by the word processor on your PC? And why bother trying to do office-style work on your Zire if you can't do it easily, efficiently, and in all the apps and formats you're used to on your desktop? With this in mind, here's a list of products you should consider if you plan to do document-editing work on your Zire:

- **E-book reader**   If you mainly want to read documents on your Zire and don't care about creating or editing them, then you can get by with a common e-book reader like Palm Reader, TealDoc, or AportisDoc—there are a lot to choose from. These programs let you read large documents that don't fit in the Zire's Memo Pad. Thousands of novels, reference books, and other documents are in the DOC format, which you can download and read on your Zire. See "The Wonderful World of E-Books" later in this chapter for the scoop on e-books.

- **Office suite**   If you want to create new documents or edit ones you made in Microsoft Office, a simple document reader isn't enough. Though office suites for the Zire are not quite full-featured—at least not in the sense that Microsoft Office on the desktop is— they programs deliver sophisticated tools like spell checkers, rich text formatting, charting tools for your spreadsheet, and more. Most importantly, these programs break through the file-size limit imposed by the Memo Pad and let you edit documents of almost unlimited length that can be shared with Word and Excel.

- **Adobe Acrobat**   If your office makes extensive use of PDF files, you should have an Acrobat reader on your Zire so you can view those documents on the go.

- **Database**   Yes, database applications are available even for the Zire. There are a slew of popular programs that let you create new databases from scratch, and most even let you import existing databases from programs like Access, FileMaker, and other ODBC-complaint applications. Some of the most popular database engines for the Zire include HanDBase, JFile, MobileDB, ThinkDB, and dbNow. FileMaker also has its own PDA "companion" to Filemaker, called (not too surprisingly) FileMaker Mobile. If you're a FileMaker user, FileMaker Mobile may be all you need. Keep in mind, though, that the Zire's 2MB memory limit means you can't do much with databases.

The Wonderful World of E-Books

You know the future has arrived when a device the size of a Pop-Tart can hold an entire Stephen King novel. Indeed, many users find electronic books (aka e-books) to be a major Zire perk. You can pay nothing at all and read hundreds of literary classics, or pay discounted prices for mainstream titles. In this chapter, you learn everything you need to know about turning your Zire into a world-class library.

Under the Hood of the Perfect Zire

Dave: My Zire is more than just a date book and contact manager. I've added just a few apps that make it a great little pocket-sized laptop replacement for the road. I updated the built-in Date Book with DateBk5, I installed WordSmith for document editing, plus I've included Palm Reader for reading e-books and Bejeweled to pass the time when a little game playing is just what I need. Those four programs make the most of the Zire's limited memory but do most of what I'd otherwise want a laptop for when I travel. What's on your Zire, Rick? A lot of Powerpuff Girl stuff, I'm guessing.

Rick: I don't even know what that means. In any case, I never leave home without Palm Reader and at least one good e-book. I'm surprised you do likewise, given that so few of those trashy romance novels you like are available in e-book form. As for fun, Astraware's Text Twist keeps me thoroughly entertained. It's one of those thinking-man's games, so you probably wouldn't like it. WordSmith works well for word processing, but I'm also fond of Quickword. It's part of the Quickoffice suite, which includes an Excel-compatible spreadsheet component.

A Brief (but Important) History of E-Books

Before handheld PCs came along, a huge collection of electronic books—mostly public-domain classic literature, like Voltaire's *Candide* and Sir Arthur Conan Doyle's *Sherlock Holmes* stories—existed on the Internet. Because these works had already been converted to computer-readable text, why not copy them to Zires for reading anytime, anywhere?

In theory, you could simply paste the text into a memo, but there's a snag: memos are limited to about 500 words, so even short stories are out of the question. Hence the emergence of one of the very first third-party Palm OS applications: *Doc*, a simple text viewer that had no length limitation other than the amount of memory in the handheld itself. Doc rapidly became the de facto standard, not only for e-books, but also for documents created in desktop word processors and converted for handhelds.

Choosing a Doc Viewer

Many people make this mistake: they download a bunch of nifty e-books from MemoWare (or wherever), load them onto their Zires, then spend lots of time trying to figure out why they can't find the books. (When you install software, there's usually an icon for it.) The reason, of course, is they don't have a Doc viewer installed. Without one, there's no way to view Doc files.

Fortunately, there are plenty of Doc viewers out there—all free or quite inexpensive. The best place to start is with Palm's own program, Palm Reader, available at **www.palmdigitalmedia.com**. What's nice about Palm Reader is that it allows you to read not only the e-books purchased from Palm Digital Media, but also Doc files you obtain elsewhere. Or you can download other readers—here's what a few common programs (Palm Reader, CSpotRun, and TealDoc) look like, side-by-side:

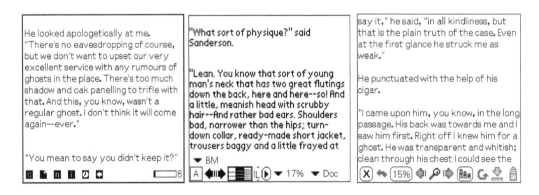

Making Room for the Books

Before we delve into the details of finding, buying, and viewing e-books, you should know that e-books can be extremely large files. Jules Verne's *The Mysterious Island,* for instance, takes a whopping 622K, while the infamous biography *Monica's Story* nabs 500K. Fortunately, not all titles are quite so gargantuan. Most short stories are under 50K, and even Stephen King's novel *The Girl Who Loved Tom Gordon* is a reasonable 226K. Even so, with only about 2MB of storage space on your Zire, you may need to delete a program or two to make room for a book you want to carry. Games tend to take up the most space, so start with those.

To delete a program from your Zire, do this:

1. Tap the Home icon to return to the main Applications screen.

2. Tap the Menu icon that's just below it, then choose Delete from the menu that appears.

3. Find the program you want to delete, tap it once to highlight it, then tap the Delete button. That's all there is to it! Now you can tap Done and move on to loading your e-book.

Free E-Books and E-Books for Sale

There are dozens of online sources for e-books, both free and commercial. The former are works considered public domain: either their copyrights have expired (as in the case of classic literature), or they've been written and released by authors not seeking compensation. There are literally thousands of titles available in the public domain, many of them already converted to the Doc format.

Commercial titles aren't unlike what you'd buy in a bookstore: they've simply been converted to an electronic format and authorized for sale online. Notice we didn't mention Doc: most commercial e-books are created using a proprietary format, meaning a special viewer is required. This is primarily to prevent unauthorized distribution—unlike actual books, commercial e-books aren't meant to be loaned out or given to others. When you buy one, you're effectively buying a license to read it on your Zire and only your Zire.

Finding Free Stuff

If one site is synonymous with Doc files, it's MemoWare (**www.memoware.com**). Here you can find thousands of texts divided into categories such as business, history, travel, biography, sci-fi,

11

Our Favorite E-Books

Rick: I've become something of an e-book zealot, recommending MemoWare and Palm Digital Media to friends, family, and any strangers who will sit still for five seconds. Among the great titles I've read on my Palm are *Angela's Ashes, Battlefield Earth, The Corrections,* and *Kick the Can.* I also enjoyed rereading *The Most Dangerous Game,* a story I remembered fondly from high school. I got that one free from MemoWare. My only hope is that Dave will one day read something that doesn't involve robots, hobbits, or robot hobbits.

Dave: I have to commend Rick on the progress he's made. When I met him a scant six years ago, he hadn't yet learned to master the written word. Since then, I've seen him get his equivalency diploma, start on "chapter books," and even sign his name in ink instead of crayon. Bravo, Rick! Well done! As for me, I find the best for the buck is the magazine *Fantasy & Science Fiction*—Palm Digital Media has a good assortment of them going back to 1997. I'm rarely disappointed by any of those tales, and there's a month's worth of bedtime reading in each collection.

and Shakespeare. Whether you're looking for a collection of Mexican recipes, a Zane Grey western, a sappy love poem, or a classic work by Dickens, this is the place to start.

MemoWare offers a convenient search engine, so you can type in a title or keyword to quickly find what you're looking for. It also has links to other e-book sites, although none are as comprehensive. Finally, MemoWare provides numerous links to software programs (most for Windows, a few for Mac) that turn computer documents into Doc files. More on that later in the chapter.

Finding Commercial Stuff

The thing about public domain e-books is that most of them are, well, old. Somerset Maugham and Jack London are all well and good for catching up on the classics you promised yourself you'd read one day, but sometimes you just want a little Stephen King. Or Mary Higgins Clark. Or Captain Kirk. Fortunately, you can have them all on your Zire, provided you're willing to pay for them.

The top place to go for contemporary, mainstream fiction and nonfiction is, without a doubt, Palm's own online bookstore, Palm Digital Media (at **www.palmdigitalmedia.com**). The site offers thousands of books from prominent authors like Stephen Ambrose, Elmore Leonard, and Anna Quindlen.

How to View Palm Digital Media Books When you purchase a book from Palm Digital Media, you supply your name and credit card number, and then receive a Zip file to download. (If you need a utility to expand Zip files, we suggest downloading WinZip from **www.winzip.com**) This file contains the e-book itself (in an encrypted .pdb format), along with the Palm Reader program. If you don't already have the Palm Reader installed on your PDA, be sure to install it before trying to read your new book.

 *When buying subsequent books, you need to install only the books themselves. You needn't install Palm Reader again.*

You also receive, via e-mail, a code number that's used to "unlock" the e-book. You need to enter this number on your Zire the first time you open your e-book.

 The code number is usually the credit card number you used to purchase the book. If you don't mind divulging it, you can indeed share the book with another handheld user. Just e-mail the file for them to install and give them the number so they can unlock the book. This is pretty smart copyright protection, if you ask us, as it allows for sharing among family members and close friends, but prevents you from giving books to strangers.

One more note about Palm Reader: you must use it to view books purchased from Palm Digital Media; no other e-book reader will let you read them. However, Palm Reader will let you view standard Doc files, such as those obtained at MemoWare and Fictionwise. Thus, it's a pretty good all-purpose program.

Other Sources for Contemporary E-Books

Palm Digital Media may be the largest source for commercial e-books, but a couple other Web sites are gaining notoriety.

- ■ **Fictionwise** Here you'll find a growing collection of fiction and nonfiction stories and novels, all of them discounted. In fact, you can buy short stories for as little as a buck—sometimes even less. One nice thing about Fictionwise is that the books are provided in the standard Doc format, so you can use your favorite Doc viewing program. (The company also recently added Palm Digital Media format books to its library, so you can read those with Palm Reader as well.) Furthermore, the site includes reader-supplied ratings for each book and story, so you can make more informed decisions on what to buy. Fictionwise also keeps a decent collection of free short stories for you to try out, so we highly recommend a visit.

- ■ **Mobipocket** This is not only an e-book content provider, but also a document viewer you can use instead of—or in addition to—Palm Reader.

Creating and Editing Documents

If you're a business traveler, you're used to carting a laptop around with you to edit Word documents. If it has a 14- or 15-inch display, then you know what it's like trying to get the screen open in the cramped space on an airplane seat. Heck, sometimes we can't get it open far enough to read what we're typing.

There's an easier solution. Your Zire can take the place of your laptop for text entry—as long as you don't mind using Graffiti or the built-in keyboard to enter text. You can even synchronize specific Word documents with your Zire, edit them on the road, and update your desktop PC with the latest versions of your work when you get home.

 *If you get really serious about doing word processing on your PDA, consider upgrading to a Palm Powered PDA that accepts external, fold-out keyboards, or check out the Pocketop Keyboard mentioned in Chapter 13.*

Using an Office Suite

Pocket PC users have one small advantage over Zire users—a Microsoft-branded office suite that includes Pocket Word and Pocket Excel. People expect those apps to be very compatible with Microsoft Office on the desktop.

What a lot of people don't realize, though, is that the broad selection of office suites for Palm Powered PDAs are at least as good as Pocket Word and Pocket Excel—sometimes more so. There are three popular suites to choose from:

- ■ **Documents to Go (www.dataviz.com)** Documents to Go is quite popular, mainly because it comes right in the box of many new Palm Powered models (but not the Zire, so don't go looking for it). In addition to a word processor (Word to Go) and spreadsheet

(Sheets to Go), the Professional edition of Documents to Go includes the ability to view (but not edit) PowerPoint slides and Adobe Acrobat (PDF) files. A feature called DocSync ensures almost 100 percent formatting preservation when you take Word files on the road, though the desktop file must start out in Word's .doc format for Word 2000 or newer.

 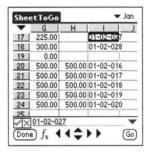

- **iambic Office (www.iambic.com)** Comprised of FastWriter and TinySheet, these programs offer Word and Excel connectivity for your Zire. In addition, the suite includes iambic Mail, an e-mail client that lets you synchronize messages with your desktop e-mail program or check mail on the go with a modem. Iambic Mail uses FastWriter and TinySheet to let you read Word and Excel attachments in e-mail.

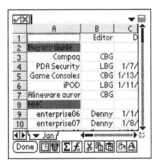 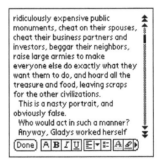

- **Quickoffice (www.cesinc.com)** This suite includes Quickword and Quicksheet for reading and editing Word and Excel documents. Quickword has its own thesaurus and spell checker, and you can install custom fonts as well.

11

> **TIP** *If you don't need the entire suite, you can usually buy the word processor and spreadsheet separately by visiting the vendor's Web site. Cutting Edge Software sells Quickword all by itself, for instance, if you don't need Quicksheet. Since your Zire has so little memory, it's probably the smarter way to go.*

Transferring Documents Between the Zire and Desktop

No matter which suite you choose, they all work more or less the same way: you use a desktop application to manage the documents you want to work with on the Zire. Just drag the document you want to move into the suite manager on the desktop, and it'll be copied to the Zire at the next HotSync. When you make a change to the document on either the Zire or the desktop, it'll be synchronized after the following HotSync, keeping the two documents exactly the same.

If you prefer not synchronize your Zire documents with their cousins on the desktop, that's fine as well. In each suite manager, you can disable synchronization and select familiar options like Handheld Overwrites, Desktop Overwrites, and Do Nothing, as you can see in Figure 11-1.

What if you create a new document from scratch on the Zire? No problem. On the next HotSync after you create the document, you'll find that it has been synchronized with the desktop. To find it, just open your suite manager software and double-click on the new file; it'll automatically open in Word.

Working with Documents and Spreadsheets

If you want to leave your laptop at home and just carry a PDA, it's absolutely essential to be able to read and edit Word and Excel files on the go. Any of the suites we've already mentioned will work, and if all you care about is text, you have a fourth excellent option as well—a program from Blue Nomad called WordSmith (pictured next). WordSmith doesn't come as part of a suite with a spreadsheet. Instead, it's a stand-alone word processor for the Zire that, like Quickoffice, includes font support, a spell checker, a thesaurus, and sophisticated formatting controls. Many users choose WordSmith as their word processor of choice, especially if they don't also need a spreadsheet.

While most Zire word processors try very hard to preserve all of the formatting in your document, keep in mind that these programs do it with varying levels of success. You may find, for instance, that group annotations or graphics like "boxes" around text may be stripped out when the files are synchronized back to the PC. As a consequence, word processing on the Zire is often best reserved for documents that have fairly conservative levels of formatting. Bottom line: since all office suites have a free trial period, we recommend installing all of them and seeing which one you like best.

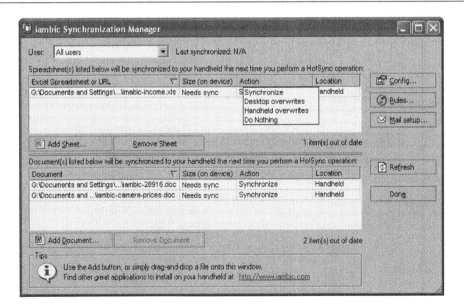

FIGURE 11-1   Most office suites let you control whether documents get synchronized between the Zire and desktop.

 **Work with Documents**

In a nutshell, here's what you need to know to work with text documents on the Zire:

- To create or edit long documents on your Zire, you need a program like Documents To Go, Quickoffice, iambic Office, or WordSmith.
- On the desktop, open your office suite's manager application.
- Click the button to add a file, or just drag and drop a document into the suite's manager's window.
- Close the program and then HotSync to transfer the files to the Zire.
- Edit the files on your Zire.
- HotSync to carry the changes you made to the Zire back to the desktop versions of the affected files.

Charts and Graphs on the Zire

Spreadsheets are often reported to be the most popular PC-based application in the history of computers (we're not sure who they talked to—personally, we'd vote for games), and like milk and cereal or guitars and rock 'n roll, nothing goes with spreadsheets quite like charts and graphs. It makes sense, then, that you might want to view your spreadsheet data visually in the form of charts and graphs, even on your Zire. You're in luck: both iambic Office and Quickoffice come with their own spreadsheet graphing tools. As you can see here, you can make some very attractive graphs using these programs.

11

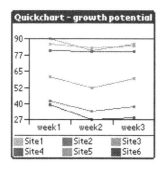 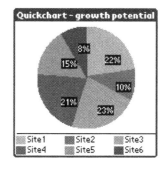

Neither of these programs is particularly intuitive, though, since they run from within their parent spreadsheet app; you won't get anywhere by tapping on TinyChart or Quickchart directly. Nonetheless, getting started with these graphing apps is easy. If you use iambic Office, just open TinySheet, select a range of cells to graph, and choose Cell | Chart from the menu. If you want to embed a chart within the spreadsheet, tap on an empty cell and choose Cell | Insert Chart instead. Then select a range of cells and draw the Enter gesture with Graffiti. Double-tap the inserted chart to view it in TinyChart.

In Quickoffice, open a spreadsheet in Quicksheet and tap on an empty cell. Then choose Chart(Range) from the list of functions. Select a range of cells for your chart, and tap in another cell or use the Enter gesture. Your chart is created. To see the finished chart, double-tap the cell that now says *CHART*. QuickChart launches, and you can modify the chart and see it in all its grayscale glory.

Adobe Acrobat on the Zire

In most offices, Word and Excel pop up pretty often—but Adobe Acrobat files, also known by their file extension as PDF files, are incredibly popular as well. That's because PDFs are self-contained, fancy-looking text-and-graphic documents that display exactly the same no matter what kind of computer you view them on. They also can't be edited, so you can distribute a PDF secure in the knowledge that some clown in room 234 won't make changes to your handiwork.

That's great, but until recently you couldn't view them on the Zire. Today, there are several ways to display Adobe Acrobat files on your PDA. Two of the better ones include

- **Documents to Go Professional**, which has its own PDF viewer. On the downside, this viewer strips out graphics, so it's only useful for documents that are text based.
- **Adobe Acrobat Reader for Palm** is a free program from Adobe that lets you download PDF files to your Zire. This program lets you choose to include or strip out graphics, so you can save memory on your PDA by leaving out nonessential graphics or leave them in if needed to understand the document.

You can find other programs that do this as well, including Microbat reader, Ansyr Primer PDF Viewer, RichReader, and PDF2Doc.

PowerPoint on your Zire

The last piece of the puzzle is PowerPoint. If you lug your laptop around so you can deliver slideshows on the road, well, we have some good news for you. Your Zire is capable of pumping slides directly to a projector—in their entire 1024×768, full-color glory. You need a little gadget called Pitch from iGo.com. Pitch connects to your HotSync cable and then goes on to attach to any standard video system, like a VGA monitor or a portable digital projector.

Actually, depending upon what you want to do with your PowerPoint slides, you have a few choices:

- **Documents to Go Professional** This program just won't go away! The professional version of DTG includes a PowerPoint viewer. You can't broadcast these slides on a projector, but you can use this viewer to view the slides in both a text-only and graphic mode.
- **Quickoffice** As we mentioned earlier, Quickoffice has a PowerPoint viewer, somewhat similar to the one in Documents to Go. Which one should you buy? It's easy: try them both. You can download free trials from the two Web sites and decide for yourself.

■ **Pitch**   If you want to plug your Zire into a projector, get Pitch. As we mentioned earlier, this gadget plugs your Zire into a projector or monitor, completely taking the place of a laptop. You can fit hundreds of slides in memory—they project in high-res and full-color—and you can avoid all of the hassles that go with setting up, booting, carrying, and managing a laptop.

Printing from Your Zire

The ultimate handheld PC would probably look a lot like your Zire, but with one important difference: it would have a paper-thin printer embedded inside, enabling you to print anything you see on the screen. While that's mere science fiction for the time being, this doesn't mean you can't print stuff from your PDA. Quite the contrary: armed with a print driver, you can send a wide variety of documents from your Zire to a desktop printer or to a portable, pocket-sized printer.

In order to print anything from your Zire, you need to add a print driver. There are four common drivers for the Palm OS, and any of these will use the Zire's infrared port to wirelessly send data to a nearby printer (as long as the printer has an infrared port as well). You can choose from

■ Instep Print

■ IrPrint

■ PalmPrint

■ PrintBoy

Infrared Printers for Your Zire

Your Zire's IR port (the same one that you can use to beam apps and data to other PDAs) can communicate directly with a small assortment of printers. If you like the idea of printing wirelessly from your Zire, or if you travel frequently and want to print from wherever you happen to be, look into one of these:

Manufacturer	Printer	Comments
Canon	BJC-50	Lightweight mobile printer
	BJC-80	Lightweight mobile printer
Datamax	E-3202	Desktop thermal printer
Hewlett-Packard	LaserJet 6P	Desktop laser printer
	LaserJet 6MP	Desktop laser printer
	LaserJet 2100	Desktop laser printer
Pentax	PocketJet 200	Lightweight mobile printer, needs optional IrDA adapter
Sipix	Pocket Printer A6	Handheld portable printer

11

What IrDA is All About

Technically, IrDA stands for the Infrared Data Association, which is just a bunch of companies that make IR-enabled products. More important, though, IrDA represents the industry-standard infrared port you can find on most laptops, handheld PCs, and printers with IR ports. If you find a printer with an IrDA port, chances are excellent it'll work with one of the Zire's print drivers.

Where to Find It

Web Site	Address	What's There
Stevens Creek	www.stevenscreek.com	PalmPrint
DataViz	www.dataviz.com	Documents To Go
Blue Nomad	www.bluenomad.com	WordSmith
Cutting Edge Software	www.cesinc.com	Quickoffice
iambic Software	www.iambic.com	iambic Office
IS/Complete	www.iscomplete.com	IRPrint and other print drivers
InStep Print	www.instepgroup.com	InStep Print
Bachmann Software	www.bachmannsoftware.com	PrintBoy and the InfraReady Adapter

Printers for Your Pocket

If you expect to do a lot of printing and want to have easy access to a portable printer, you have a few excellent choices. Forget about having to track down a desktop printer when you're on the road—just carry your printer in your pocket. Here are two models we highly recommend:

- The Sipix Pocket Printer A6 is a lightweight printer that measures just 6 × 4 × 1 inches; it's literally small enough to fit in your hand. It uses a thermal process to print on a roll of paper at about 400dpi. The Pocket Printer runs on four AA batteries and has both a serial interface and an IrDA port, which means you can print wirelessly.

- The Pentax PocketJet is a bit longer—it's 10 × 2 × 1 inches and uses thermal imaging to print 300dpi on either sheets or rolls of paper. The Pentax may be bigger, but it lets you print real letter-sized documents. It, too, uses serial and IrDA, and it uses AC power or internal rechargeable batteries for power.

Chapter 12

Games and Music

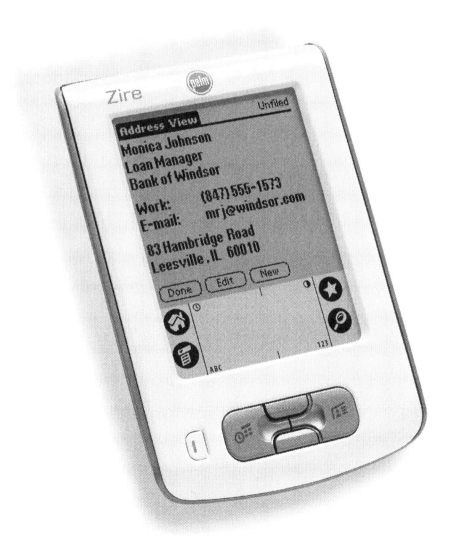

How to...

- Play games on your Zire
- Adjust the Zire's volume for games
- Find and install new games
- Use the Zire as a substitute for dice
- Sketch and doodle on your Zire
- Turn your Zire into a metronome
- Find software to help you master the piano or guitar
- Compose music on your Zire

Spreadsheets, databases, and memos are all well and good. If that's all you ever plan to do with your Zire, that's fine—you're just unlikely to ever get invited to one of our parties. Time to break out and have some fun with your handheld, to play some fun games and perhaps even make a little music.

Turn Your Zire into a Game Machine

No, playing games isn't exactly rocket science, but before you get started with them, you should learn a few things that'll come in handy. You should know, for instance, how to find games online, download them to your computer, install them on your Zire, and adjust your Zire's volume control.

Control the Zire's Game Volume

The Zire has a volume control that's expressly for games. Logic dictates you'll want to set this loud enough to hear what's going on in your game, but this might not always be the case. As much as we like to play games, we don't always want others to know that's what we're doing. Fortunately, it's possible to set the game sound level low or even off completely. This means you'll play your games without sound (which, if you're at work, is probably a wise decision).

To tweak game volume, do this:

1. Tap the Prefs icon to open your Preferences application.
2. Switch to the General category by tapping on the category menu at the upper-right corner and choosing General.
3. Find the Game Sound entry and choose the volume level you're interested in.

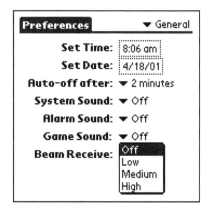

> **TIP**
> *If you play a game that squeaks and squawks even if the sound is off, the game must have its own sound preferences. Check the game's menu for a preferences control to set the sound volume. Indeed, many games have built-in volume controls that eliminate the need to futz around with the settings in Prefs.*

Download and Install Games

There are several ways to obtain games for your Zire. Your local office supply or computer store may carry some Palm game collections, which usually pack several—or even dozens—of games into a single box. These are nice because the games are right at your fingertips—no Web surfing or downloading required. However, if you're adept enough with a PC to browse a few Web sites and download a few files, you can find most (if not all) of the same games online. You won't pay any money for them, either.

> **TIP**
> *This does not necessarily mean the games are free, though some are. Most of the game collections sold in stores contain shareware—or trial—versions of various games. These versions may allow you to play only a certain number of times or have certain features disabled. To "unlock" the game, you have to pay for a registration code, but if you buy a game collection, you're paying twice: once for the CD that contains the games, and again for the actual game when you register it. That's why we usually recommend people skip the collections and download games from the Web.*

So, where you can find games online? There are lots of sites that have them, but we recommend these three destinations:

- Handango (**www.handango.com**)
- Palm Gaming World (**www.palmgamingworld.com**)
- PalmGear (**www.palmgear.com**)

12

Installing Games on Your Zire

Installing games is a snap. We discussed how to install applications on your Zire in Chapter 4, and working with games is no different. After all, a game is just another kind of Zire program.

If you're new to downloading applications from the Internet, you need to know that most apps come compressed in one of two popular formats:

- **Zip** This is the standard way of managing files in Windows. A "zipped" file is compressed, usually to make it smaller (and, therefore, faster to download) but also so it can include multiple files (the application, instructions, and whatever else might be necessary). To open a zipped file, you need a program capable of unzipping it first. We recommend WinZip, which is available free from **www.winzip.com**. (This isn't necessary for Windows XP users, as that operating system can automatically extract the contents of Zip files.)

- **Sit** Macintosh files are compressed in the SIT format, which can be uncompressed with a program like Aladdin Stuffit Expander 5.0.

Once expanded, you'll probably have a folder with several files in it. Installation instructions typically come in one or more file formats:

- **Plain text files** Usually called something clever like readme.txt or install.txt.
- **Web pages** Double-click them to see the directions in your Web browser.
- **Adobe Acrobat files** These end with the PDF file extension. You need Adobe Acrobat to read these files, though it's probably already installed on your computer. If not, visit **adobe.com** to get this popular document reader.

Finally, there should be one or more files with PRC and PDB extensions. These are the actual game files that need to be installed on your Zire. Open the Install tool and use the Add button to set these files for installation at the next HotSync.

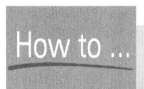
Control the Games

Now you're all set to start playing some Zire games—but where's the joystick? There isn't one, silly. Many games require nothing more than tapping on the screen, while others rely on the Zire's buttons to control the action. While the game is running, the Date Book, Address Book, and sometimes Scroll buttons are diverted to game controls and won't function as they normally do. However, you may encounter a Zire-related limitation in games that make use of more than two buttons: most Palm handhelds have four application buttons instead of two, and some games take advantage of them. Such games—there aren't too many, fortunately—probably won't be playable on your Zire.

 *If you use WinZip, a faster way to install games is simply to drag the PRC and PDB files from the WinZip window into the Install Tool dialog box (they'll dynamically expand as you drag them, meaning you needn't manually unzip the files into a folder on your hard disk), or try double-clicking the PRC and/or PDB files from within WinZip.*

 Need to pause a game? Just turn off your Zire or switch to another application. In most cases, the game remains frozen until you turn it back on again.

Using the Zire as a Pair of Dice

If you like to play board games in the real world, you might be interested in using your Zire as a virtual pair of dice. After all, the Zire is harder to lose (we always misplace the dice that go with our board games). And if you play role-playing games like Dungeons & Dragons, you'll appreciate these programs' ability to "roll" a wide variety of dice—not just the usual six-sided cube. We recommend DicePro, Gamers Die Roller, and Roll Em, all of which are available from PalmGear.com.

```
┌─────────────────────────────────────┐
│ Roll Em                              │
│ Total      13  S-Rolls        8      │
│ Sum        13  S-Dice        18      │
│ Mean        4  S-Tot         70      │
│     ©      Best 3 of 4d6     ®       │
│   ┌────────────┐  ┌────────────┐     │
│   │    1d2     │  │    1d4     │     │
│   ├────────────┤  ├────────────┤     │
│   │    1d6     │  │    1d8     │     │
│   ├────────────┤  ├────────────┤     │
│   │   1d10     │  │   1d12     │     │
│   ├────────────┤  ├────────────┤     │
│   │   1d20     │  │   1d100    │     │
│   └────────────┘  └────────────┘     │
│   ⏴ ⏵  1      │ Custom │             │
└─────────────────────────────────────┘
```

The Universe of Zire Games

Games account for a pretty healthy chunk of all software sold for handheld PCs, so it should come as no surprise that you can find hundreds upon hundreds of titles spanning every genre. Card games, action games, puzzle games—you name it, it's out there. Of course, we can't list all of them without doubling the size of the book. It's big enough already, don't you think?

As with other kinds of Zire software, games are easy to try before you buy. Most have a trial period, usually from two weeks to a month, after which the game becomes disabled unless you register it (that is, pay for a code to unlock it permanently). Games usually cost from $10–20, though a few will set you back $30. There's also a treasure trove of great freebies like these (all of them available at **www.freewarepalm.com**):

- ■ **Mulg II**   Use your stylus to guide a marble through a maze within a fixed amount of time. Devilishly addictive.
- ■ **PilOth**   A clone of the classic game of Othello.

- **Sea War** A nice implementation of the beloved game Battleship.
- **Solitaire Poker** One of many variations on Solitaire, this one involving poker hands.
- **Vexed 2.0** One of the most addictive puzzle games ever, and a Palm OS freeware classic. The 2.0 version includes seven puzzle packs with over 400 levels. Here's what the game looks like:

In the following sections, we clue you in on the various kinds of games you can get for your Zire and tell you about some of our favorites.

Card and Board Games

Games based on paper and cardboard—board games, card games, games of chance—transition well to the Zire because they're games you can relax with, take your time with, and return to after the dentist calls your name. Poker, Hearts, Blackjack, Yahtzee, Scrabble, Monopoly, chess, checkers—there are versions of just about every classic card and board game you can think of.

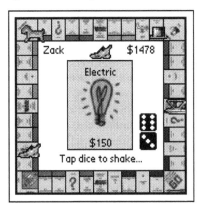

*Where to find these and other games? We've already told you countless times about Handango and PalmGear, so we won't do that again. Instead, try Palm Gaming World (**www.palmgamingworld.com**), a site devoted entirely to—you guessed it—games for the Palm OS.*

Puzzle Games

We love puzzles. Many puzzle games for the Zire come from the PC and other traditional gaming sources. You'll probably recognize Tetris, for instance, the classic game of falling blocks, but you'll also find far more advanced puzzle games, which represent some of our all-time favorites for the Zire. We're talking about titles like Bejeweled, Collapse, NetWalk, and Vexed. The latter is freeware, making it a definite must-have for your handheld. Many of the others come from Astraware, makers of some of the absolute best puzzle games.

Strategy and Role-Playing Games

For those folks who want a compromise between the frenetic pace of arcade games and the cerebral thrill of interactive fiction, there's role playing and action-strategy. These games let you don some armor and go fight for gold, glory, or the king's honor. One of the most popular games in this genre is Kyle's Quest, a title for which you can download dozens of add-on adventures. If you're nostalgic for Dungeons and Dragons, there's Dragon Bane (see Figure 12-1), a classic dungeon, puzzle, and combat title.

12

| FIGURE 12-1 | If you're into role-playing games, check out Dragon Bane. It's like the classic PC game Bard's Tale. |

Sketch and Draw on Your Zire

In Chapter 8 you learned the wonders of Note Pad, the handy little scratchpad program that comes with your Zire. Of course, it's a bit rudimentary, which is why you might want to consider a more robust alternative. With the programs we discuss in this section, you can draw a map to someone's house, outline a process, or design a flow chart. You can also just doodle, using the Zire as a high-tech Etch-a-Sketch for those boring times when you're waiting for the train or pretending to take notes in a meeting.

Although the Zire's monochrome, low-resolution screen doesn't lend itself to much more than basic sketching and doodling, there are programs that offer a wider array of features than Note Pad. Some give you lots of drawing tools, others let you add alarms to your drawings, and so on.

■ **TealPaint** Perhaps the most full-featured paint program for the Zire, TealPaint does it all. The program has a complete set of painting tools, including lines, shapes, fill tools, an eraser, and a variety of brushes.

- **Diddle** Diddle is a neat little drawing program that enables you to sketch with a minimum of clutter to get in the way of your drawing. The interface is composed of a set of graphical menus at the top of the screen—you can choose from among various drawing styles, line thickness, and text. For the most part, the program is easy to explore on your own—just start drawing. Best of all, it's free!

- **BugMe** More than just a scratchpad, BugMe advances the notion of turning your Zire screen into an electronic Sticky Note. Thus, you can not only make quick sketches (using a variety of tools), but also turn any note into a "visual alarm." That is, you set an alarm for a note, and when your Zire beeps, the note appears on the screen.

Collaborate on a Sketch

12

Drawing on a Zire is usually a solo affair, but what if you're in a meeting trying to lay out office furniture with your business partner? What then, huh? Okay, there may be some better examples, but just work with us for a moment.

Okay, we have a better example! Suppose you're in a long, boring meeting. If you have the right drawing software, you can doodle on your Zire and have it immediately show up on a partner's Zire (or another Palm OS handheld). Your partner can then add to your drawing and beam it back to you. All the while, your boss is none the wiser.

Anyway, if your buddy, business partner, or intern owns another Palm OS handheld, the two of you can sketch your ideas together. The results can appear simultaneously in both devices more or less in real time. That's totally cool, if you ask us.

Most collaborative sketch programs do their magic via the Zire's IR port. Here are some popular programs you can try:

- **Beamer** This simple program has just a few buttons but it's free. You can write short notes in a screen that resembles the Note Pad or draw free-form images in a blank sketchpad. When you're ready, tap the Beam button (it looks like a tilde sign) to beam it to another nearby handheld. The recipient can add to your drawing and beam it back.

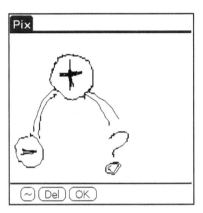

■ **Zapster** Very similar to Beamer, this program has a slightly more elegant interface. On the downside, it's shareware and costs $10. Like Beamer, you use it to draw and then beam your work to another handheld, where it can be edited and returned.

Make Music on Your Zire

Believe it or not, you can use the Zire for a number of music applications. It has a built-in speaker for creating (admittedly, very basic) sounds, and the display is perfectly suited for music notation in a small space. If you're a musician, be sure to check out some of these applications.

Metronome and Drumming Software

It doesn't take a rocket scientist to figure out the Zire's sound capabilities aren't exactly symphonic in nature, but it's certainly adept enough to keep time, either as a drum machine or a metronome. In fact, this would have come in handy a long time ago, when Dave used to carry a guitar wherever he went. Having a metronome or mini-drum machine in a device as small as the Zire would have been really cool.

■ **Meep** This is your standard metronome. Meep has a slider for choosing any tempo from 40 to 280 beats per minute, and you can select up to 8 beats per measure as well. You can work from onscreen counts or add an audible beep to each beat.

■ **Responsive Metronome** Another simple metronome tool, Responsive Metronome enables you to choose any tempo from 35 to 300 beats per minute, and both see (via a pulsing quarter note) and hear the beat. This program is quite simple and, in fact, there's no on/off switch for the beat—you have to disable both the audio and video filters to shut it off.

■ **Pocket Beat** This app simulates a drum kit right on your Zire. It can remember two distinct tempos, and you can switch between them easily by using onscreen controls or the Scroll button. Pocket Beat can also play straight or shuffle beats, and it can vary between 40 and 196 beats per minute. The best part, though, is you can tap out your own meter on the Zire screen—Pocket Beat memorizes the tempo and plays it accordingly.

Here you can see images from Meep, Responsive Metronome, and PocketBeat:

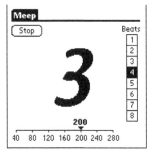  

Portable Music Lessons

Budding musicians can carry around the following applications with them to bone up on notes, keyboard positions, and fingering:

■ **GTrainer** If you're learning to play guitar and you don't want to be forever tied to "tab" sheet music, try GTrainer. This program displays a note onscreen, and you need to tap the correct place on the guitar fretboard. It isn't enough just to choose the right note—you have to tap the correct octave as well.

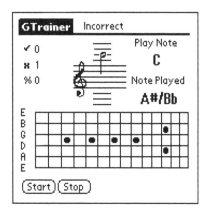

12

■ **McChords** If you're learning piano, McChords is an essential portable tool for working through chord fingerings. It shows you which keys to press to form the majority of chords you need to master basic piano playing.

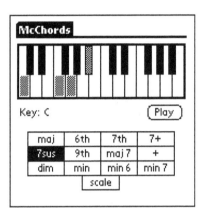

■ **PChord** This program is indispensable for anyone trying to get the hang of the guitar. In fact, PChord also supports mandolin, banjo, violin, and other stringed instruments. Choose a chord and PChord displays a variety of ways to finger it. PChord includes every chord we could think of, including obscure (minor 9th and stacked fourths) chords you might play only once in a great while. As such, it's a good memory jogger even for experienced players.

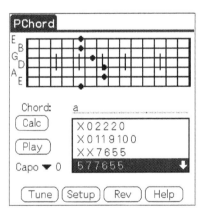

Tools for Musicians

Several programs are around to help you tune your instruments. We're not sure we'd rely on the Zire for instrument tuning, but you can certainly try these apps and see if they do the job for you:

- ■ **Guitar Tuner Lt**   Guitar Tuner Lt is great for tuning a guitar. Dave has used it himself on several occasions. It comes with standard and alternative tunings. Tap the appropriate onscreen string, and the tone plays for several seconds, or tap the Auto button to hear each string's tone in turn.

- ■ **Musician Tools**   This application is easily one of the best all-around utilities for the Zire-wielding musician. Musician Tools combines three utilities into a single interface and does them all well. You'll find a metronome that varies in temp from 40 to 210 beats per minute and one to eight beats per measure. The output is both audible and visual. (Other metronome tools are described earlier in this chapter.) An excellent tuning fork also emits a tone for various notes and a number of base frequencies. Finally, the program includes a circle of fifths.

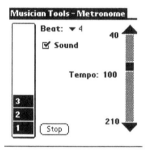 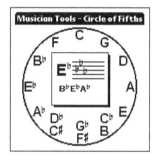 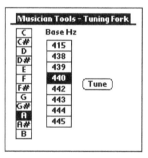

Music Annotation and Recording

You may have tried applications on the Mac or PC that enable you to compose and play music. Those programs generally let you drag notes onto musical staffs or play an onscreen keyboard to construct musical compositions. Well, you can do the same thing on the Zire—the screen is just a bit smaller, and you don't have multiple voices to hear your creations. Here are a few applications you can try:

- ■ **TS Noter**   This unusually named program is an online favorite because it's so good at helping you create music. TS Noter features a staff and a set of tools for placing notes and rests. When you create your song, you can save it, play it, or even export it as an alarm for the Zire's Date Book. A desktop companion program lets you play the music you create on your Zire from a PC using a MIDI instrument.

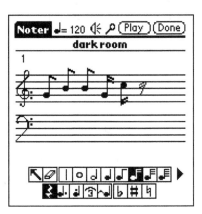

■ **miniPiano**   This program enables you to play an onscreen keyboard while the notes you strike get added on a staff. You can then play back your creation. miniPiano has a Free Play mode in which the keys are duration sensitive—the longer you hold the stylus on the key, the longer it plays.

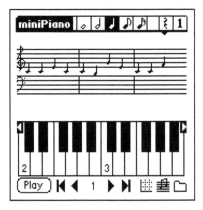

■ **Palm Piano**   This simple program records the notes you tap out on a four-octave keyboard, and it can play back the results. Palm Piano has some simple editing tools built in, but it doesn't have rests, and there's no way to select note lengths—they all play back at the same timing.

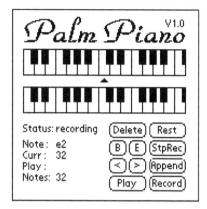

■ **PocketSynth**   Like Palm Piano, this program enables you to create music by tapping on an onscreen keyboard. PocketSynth enables you to select note lengths and rests, though, which gives you more composing flexibility. Unfortunately, you must select the length of the note and then tap it on the keyboard, which makes the composition process less than entirely fluid.

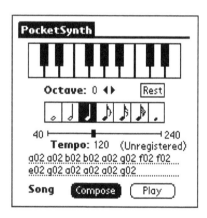

12

Where to Find It

Web Site	Address	What's There
WinZip	www.winzip.com	WinZip file compression tool for Windows
Aladdin Systems	www.aladdinsys.com	Stuffit Expander file compression tool for the Mac
Palm Gaming World	www.palmgamingworld.com	One-stop surfing for all sorts of games for the Zire
PalmGear	www.palmgear.com	Games, music software, and other Palm OS programs
Handango	www.handango.com	Games, music software, and other Palm OS programs

Chapter 13

Graffiti Enhancements and Other Utilities

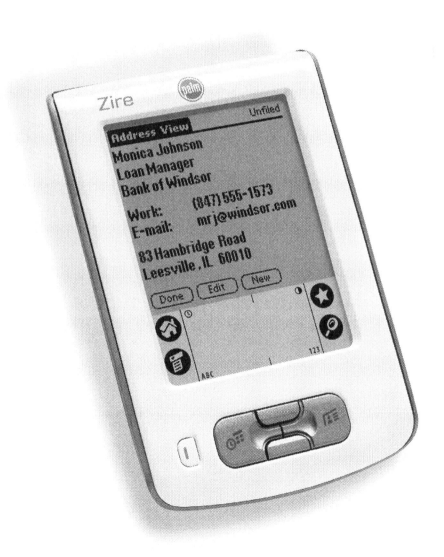

How to...

- Install and use Hacks
- Make capital letters the easy way
- Automatically correct spelling errors
- Drag and drop text
- Automatically remove duplicate entries from your databases
- Manage and beam applications
- Choose a launcher
- Make the Graffiti area more functional
- Replace Graffiti with a different handwriting recognition engine
- Replace the built-in keyboard with other keyboards
- Write anywhere on the Zire's screen
- Take advantage of "digital ink"
- Write faster with word-completion software

When life gives you lemons, make lemonade, and when your Zire gives you grief because of something it does (or doesn't do), give it a utility. Utilities are little programs that fix, enhance, add, or replace certain functions. This can be anything from an improved onscreen keyboard to a program launcher designed to keep your icons orderly and accessible. In this chapter, we look at some neat and practical ways to tweak your Zire.

X-Master and the Wonderful World of "Hacks"

The mother of all Zire utilities, *X-Master* is what separates the men from the boys, the women from the girls. It's a tool Tim Allen would love, as it allows Zires to reach beyond their limits, to achieve "more power!" It's a tool many users come to find indispensable.

What X-Master Does

Technically speaking, X-Master is an "operating system extension manager." By itself, it serves no function, but it enables the use of *Hacks*—little programs that extend the capabilities of your Zire. Forget the negative connotations usually associated with "hacking"—these programs are here to help, not harm.

And if you want to run them, you must first download and install X-Master. See Chapter 4 for information on installing programs like this—it's applicable to the Hacks you'll be downloading as well.

 *Because Hacks tinker directly with the Palm OS, they can create the occasional glitch, and the more Hacks you have installed and running, the greater the likelihood of some sort of problem. The most common is your Zire crashing, which is usually more of an annoyance than anything else.*

As you venture out into the world of Palm OS software, you may discover other Hack managers. For instance, there's *HackMaster,* the granddaddy that started this whole crazy Hack business (but we don't recommend using HackMaster, as it's an older program and slightly buggy when used on a Zire). There's also *TealMaster,* the most robust and feature-rich of all the Hack managers. But we're partial to X-Master because we've used it extensively, and it has just the features we need. Plus, it's freeware—unlike TealMaster, which costs $9.95.

How to Use It

Launching X-Master is no different from launching any other program—you just tap its icon, but, as previously noted, the software is useless without any Hacks loaded. Therefore, to help you learn to use this utility, we're going to walk you through the installation of one of our favorite Hacks.

It's called *MiddleCaps,* and it saves you from having to write the Graffiti upstroke every time you want to create an uppercase letter. Instead, you simply write the letter so it crosses the invisible line between the letter and number sides of the Graffiti area. We find this enables us to write much more quickly and naturally.

MiddleCaps is freeware, as many Hacks are, so you can download and use it free of charge. (A note of appreciation e-mailed to the author is always nice.) You can find MiddleCaps at PalmGear, among other sites. Let's get it running on your Zire.

1. Download MiddleCaps and install it on your Zire. (Remember, you should have already installed X-Master first.) You won't find an icon for MiddleCaps—or any other Hack— in the Applications screen. The only real evidence of Hacks appears in X-Master.

2. Tap the X-Master icon to load the utility, and you'll see MiddleCaps listed.

3. Notice the empty box to the left of the name. Tap it with your stylus and you'll see a check mark appear. That means the Hack is now enabled. If you want to disable it, just tap the box again. (For purposes of our tutorial, please leave it enabled.)

4. Notice the Configure button at the bottom of the screen. Tap it to set up MiddleCaps (a one-time procedure).

5. You're now in the MiddleCaps Preferences screen, where you can tweak a few of the program's settings. For now, check the box marked Caps On Crossing. This means a capital letter will appear whenever you write a character that crosses between the letter and number sides of the Graffiti area. You can test it by tapping to place your cursor on the line near the bottom of the screen and then doing some sample writing.

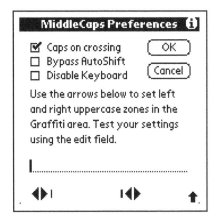

Tap OK to return to the main X-Master screen. That's it! MiddleCaps is now enabled and will work in all Palm OS applications—even third-party ones.

What about those other two buttons at the bottom of the X-Master screen? You can tap Details to get version information and other notes about the Hack or tap Info to get the Hack's "splash screen."

Important Notes About X-Master

You need to abide by a few rules of thumb when using X-Master on your Zire, all of them intended to keep things running smoothly:

■ If you ever decide to delete a Hack from your Zire, make sure you disable it first! If you try to delete a Hack while it's still running, it could causes errors, crashes, or even data loss.

■ If you install two or three Hacks on your Zire, don't enable them all simultaneously. Instead, enable one at a time, making sure it works properly before enabling the next one.

■ If you have to reset your Zire for any reason, a message pops up asking if you want to "reinstall your formerly active collection of system Hacks." Tap Reinstall (the equivalent of "yes") only if you're sure it wasn't a Hack that forced you to have to reset in the first place. Otherwise, tap Cancel. Then you can go back into X-Master and manually enable your Hacks again.

World's Greatest Hacks

If you were impressed by what MiddleCaps did for your Zire, wait till you get a load of some of our other favorites. Rather than list them by name, which doesn't always express what they do, we're going to list them by function. You can find all these Hacks at PalmGear.

Automatically Correct Spelling Errors

Giving Graffiti a helping hand, *CorrectHack* works like the AutoCorrect feature in Microsoft Word, automatically correcting words you frequently misspell. Alas, it doesn't have a database of its own; you have to supply both the words and their correct spellings, but as you compile your list over time, you'll wind up with far fewer mistakes. Also, you can also use CorrectHack as shorthand for commonly used words. For instance, you write your initials, and the software automatically plugs in your full name.

Fonts…Lots and Lots of Fonts

The Palm OS comes with a whopping three fonts: regular, bold, and large. That's not nearly enough for those of us who grew up with Arial, Century Gothic, Times New Roman, and other font faves. You can have access to a boatload of typefaces if you install *FontHack 123,* which lets you replace the system fonts with fonts of your choosing. FontHack comes with just one—you'll find 20 more in the Alpha Font Collection 1.71. Both products are freeware. Beat that!

Drag and Drop Text

While you can select snippets of text by tapping and dragging your stylus, you can't drag that text to another spot and drop it in (as you can with any word processor). *TextEditHack* adds that capability to text-oriented applications like Memo Pad and even makes it easier to select text. You can double-tap to select a single word, triple-tap to select a sentence, and quadruple-tap to select all the text on the screen. Very handy.

Enhance the Find Feature

FindHack turbocharges the Zire's Find function, remembering the last six searches you performed and letting you define up to four default searches. What's more, you can choose whether to search all installed applications, just the core apps, or only the currently loaded program. It even supports the use of wildcards—searching for "book*" would return "book," "bookmark," "bookstore," and so forth.

Look Up a Contact Without Switching Programs

While the Palm makes it easy to switch back and forth between programs, it can be a hassle to have to quit what you're doing just to look up, say, a phone number or address. *PopUp Names* pulls up your address book "on top" of the program that's currently running—and with a handy two-paned window. Thus, it's not only a timesaver, it's also a more practical way of accessing your contact list.

Improve Your Graffiti Accuracy

One of our all-time favorite hacks is *TealEcho,* which lets you see your Graffiti strokes as you write them. This "visual feedback" helps you improve your writing speed and accuracy, as it lets you see how your characters really look, then tweak your writing style so you make them correctly. TealEcho costs $11.95, but we think it's well worth the money. We tell you about some other neat Graffiti enhancements later in this chapter.

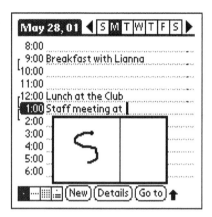

Liven Up Those Sound Effects

Getting tired of your handheld's boring old beeps? *TechSounds* comes with a handful of nifty audio snippets you can assign to various system functions, and enables you to download even more sound effects (**www.ecamm.com**). It also supports startup and shutdown screens, if you're into that sort of thing.

Other Utilities

X-Master works minor miracles, but it isn't the only tool you should consider owning. No Hacks can create reliable backups of your data or remove duplicate entries from your databases. So read on to learn about some of the other highlights of the Palm OS utility world.

Most of the utilities listed here can be purchased and downloaded from Handango or PalmGear.

13

Make a Bulletproof Backup

One of the really cool things about the Palm OS is the way it keeps a complete copy of your data on your PC. Every time you HotSync, it's like you're making a backup of your important info. If something terrible befalls your handheld—it gets lost, stolen, run over, sat on, or inexplicably wiped clean—at least you know your data lives on your PC.

Ah, but what about all the extra programs you've installed and the data files that go with them? Blue Nomad's *BackupBuddy* creates a backup of every bit of data on your Zire, programs and preferences included, every time you HotSync. Doesn't the Palm OS do that? Well, yes and no. While the Palm OS does back up most of your programs and data, it doesn't necessarily catch

The Problem with Prequels

Zire, schmire. . . let's talk about the really important stuff—namely, treasured sci-fi franchises that have been ruined by prequels.

Rick: First there was the colossal disappointment of *Enterprise,* the blandest, most uninteresting *Star Trek* series ever. Now, George Lucas continues to make a mockery of the *Star Wars* trilogy by serving up pabulum like *Attack of the Clones.* Maybe I'm too old, maybe I'm jaded, maybe I just expect fresh writing and decent acting, but these prequels have left me colder than a polar bear in January. They're just not *fun.* The magic is gone. I think this is a problem inherent to the prequel formula—when you know the outcome, there's no suspense. I *know* Anakin will turn into Darth Vader in *Episode III.* For me there's no excitement in watching it happen, and don't get me started on all the ways *Enterprise* has violated *Star Trek* canon. . .

Dave: You, my friend, have been abducted by mind-controlling body snatchers. First, *Enterprise*: it's fresh, fun, and engaging. I enjoy the show immensely, though I'm sometimes disappointed that the stories are too "*Next Generation*-ish." It's always with the time travel, and there's often not enough "gee whiz, Batman! We're in outer space!" As for Lucas's *Episode II,* you're just off your rocker. Are you too cool to like stuff anymore? All the million-dollar book royalties gone to your head? What do you expect? To be knocked off your feet like you were watching *Star Wars* when you were 12? Not going to happen—that film is a classic, and you were lucky enough to see it for the first time at the perfect age. *Episode II* is a good film in its own right, though, and it may eventually be judged as the second best of the lot . . . unless *Episode III* really knocks our socks off.

everything. Technical details aside, if you want a 100-percent backup, BackupBuddy does the job, and if your handheld ever gets completely wiped, a regular old HotSync is all it takes to restore everything.

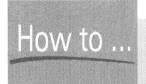 **Beam Software to Another Palm User**

Suppose you're enjoying a game of Vexed (one of our favorites), and a fellow Zire user says, "Hey, I'd like to try that!" Generous sort that you are, you agree to beam a copy of the game (which is perfectly legal because Vexed is freeware). To do so, return to the Applications screen (by tapping the Home icon) and choose Menu | App | Beam. Find Vexed in the software list, tap to highlight it, and tap the Beam button. Point your Zire at the other person's Zire, and then wait a few seconds for the transfer to complete. Presto! You've just shared some great software—wirelessly!

Extend the Clipboard with Clipper

Like most computers, Zires make use of a "clipboard" for copying and pasting text, and, like most computers, Zires can hold only one selection of text at a time in that clipboard. *Clipper* turns it into a repository for multiple selections, thereby expanding your copying-and-pasting capabilities. Everything you copy is retained in Clipper (where you can even go in and edit the text). When you want to paste something, you simply make a special Graffiti stroke to bring up the Clipper window and then choose which snippet of text to paste.

This can come in extremely handy if you frequently write the same lengthy words or phrases. Doctors could use Clipper to create a little database of diagnoses, lawyers to maintain a selection of legal terms, and so on. Sure, you could use the Zire's own ShortCuts feature (see Chapter 9) to do much the same thing, but that requires you to remember every shortcut abbreviation.

Manage (and Beam!) Your Files with Filez

The more you work with software, the more you need a good file manager. *Filez* lets you view, edit, copy, move, delete, and beam virtually any file on your handheld. It's not the most user-friendly program of its kind, but it does have one feature that makes up for it: it's free.

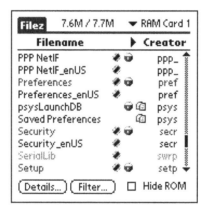

Beaming is one of Filez's most admirable capabilities. As you may recall from Chapter 4, beaming programs and data to other Zire users isn't only practical, it's just plain fun, but the Palm OS is a bit limited in terms of what it can beam. Specifically, it can't beam Hacks or e-books or certain kinds of databases. That's where Filez comes in—it can beam just about anything.

Organize Icons with a Launcher

As you know from poring over Chapter 2 (you did pore, didn't you?), the Palm OS enables you to assign applications to different categories—the idea being to help keep your icons organized and more easily accessible. However, a variety of third-party programs take this idea to a much

13

higher level and with much better results. In this section, we introduce you to a few of our favorite launchers—programs that organize your apps, simplify certain features, and, in some cases, slap on a much prettier interface.

A Few of Our Favorite Launchers

We've tried most of the launchers out there, including the one that attempts to re-create the—horrors—Windows desktop on your handheld's screen. Rest assured, that one isn't among our favorites (but if the idea intrigues you, by all means check it out—it's called GoBar). These are

 *As with most Zire software, you can try demo versions of these launchers before plunking down your hard-earned cash. We recommend you use each one for at least a week so you can really get to know it.*

- **Launch 'Em** It's not the most stylish-looking launcher we've seen, but *Launch 'Em* does have simplicity and flexibility in its corner. The software uses a tabbed interface to organize your icons, so you can switch categories with a single tap of the stylus. It costs $14.95.

- **SilverScreen** Dave's launcher of choice, *SilverScreen* offers the most glamorous interface of any launcher and a growing library of way-cool themes. It's also the only launcher to replace the core-app icons with icons of its own, thus creating an even more customized look. In short, if you're big on bells and whistles, this is the launcher for you. However, we should point out that SilverScreen is a bit on the slow side—the unfortunate by-product of its graphics-laden interface.

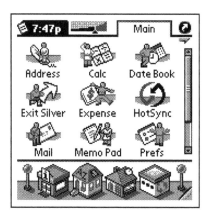

Graffiti Enhancements and Alternatives

Many of us have a love/hate relationship with Graffiti, the handwriting-recognition software used by the Zire (and all Palm OS handhelds). Some users take to it right away, finding it a speedy and convenient method for entering data. Others just plain don't like it or can't get the knack. For those folks (who have absolutely nothing to be ashamed of, really), we present this section on Graffiti enhancements and alternatives.

 **Add More Memory to Your Zire**

13

Think you're turning into a Zire power user? Hey, it's inevitable after reading this book. And maybe you've discovered that the Zire's 2MB of memory just aren't enough. Must you buy a whole new handheld to get more? Not if you're willing to part with your Zire for a few days. Just send it off to STNE Corp. (**www.stnecorp.com**) and they'll upgrade it to 8MB. At press time, the price for this service was $49.95. That's probably about half what you paid for the Zire—but it's still less expensive than a new handheld. Of course, if you're really turning into a power user, it may make sense to buy something with a bit more power.

 *One of our favorite tips for Zire users is to apply a piece of Scotch 811 Magic Tape to the Graffiti area. This not only protects the area from scratches, it also adds a tackier writing surface that many people find preferable to the slippery screen. Once the tape starts to wear out, you can simply remove it and apply another piece. One $3 roll of the stuff will last you a lifetime.*

Graffiti Overlays

The entire Graffiti area—buttons and all—is sensitive to pressure. That's why when you tap a button or write something with your stylus, your Zire responds. Overlays simply take advantage of this fact, using special software to reprogram the Zire's responses to your taps and strokes. Two products—*Silkyboard* and *TapPad*—take different approaches to this, as you see in our overview of each one.

Have Your Keyboard and Graffiti, Too

If you often hop between Graffiti and the built-in keyboard and find yourself wishing you had an easier way to do so, Softava's Silkyboard is the answer. This overlay covers the Graffiti area with a large, easy-to-read QWERTY keyboard that enables full-time tap-typing, but also lets you use Graffiti without having to change modes.

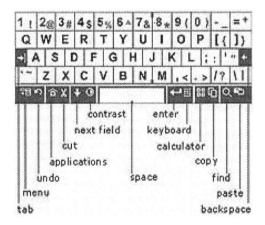

Silkyboard's key advantage is it provides access to a keyboard without sacrificing any screen estate. Its secondary advantage is protection of the Graffiti area. Working with the overlay is as simple as tapping on the letter or number you want to enter, and holding down your stylus for a "long tap" when you want a capital letter or punctuation mark. Accessing Applications, Menu, Calc, and Find requires a stroke instead of a tap, but that's just a matter of simple memorization. Indeed, Silkyboard's learning curve is slight, and, if you get mixed up, you can go back to using Graffiti just by drawing the strokes on top of the letters. (The overlay even has the two little arrows that divide the letter and number areas.)

Given that different handhelds have slightly different Graffiti areas, Silkyboard is available in several varieties. Make sure you order the one that's designed for the Zire. A simple calibration routine is all that's required to set up the driver software, and a handy applicator strip is provided to make sure the overlay is applied without any air bubbles.

If you prefer to write with a keyboard but don't want to give up Graffiti entirely, Silkyboard is a great best-of-both-worlds solution.

Make Graffiti Smarter

One of the most ingenious overlays is TapPad, which doesn't try to replace or revamp Graffiti, but merely gives it a boost. TapPad extends the full length of the Graffiti area, thus providing total protection.

TapPad's benefits can be summed up thusly:

- Protection of the Graffiti area and a tackier surface that makes handwriting more comfortable.

- The addition of a keypad in the numeric half, enabling you to enter addresses and phone numbers much more quickly (and more easily, in our opinion).

- One-tap buttons for six commonly used commands: Undo, Cut, Copy, Paste, Delete, and Backspace. The Undo button alone is worth the price of admission.

- Left-right and up-down scroll buttons for easier cursor movement and document navigation. If you've ever tried to place your cursor in between two letters or at the beginning of a line, you know what a struggle it can be. The left-right buttons move your cursor one space at a time, greatly simplifying its placement. And the up-down scroll buttons are a major improvement over the Zire's skinny scroll bars and tiny arrows.

- A host of shortcut and pop-up tools designed to simplify data entry. Space doesn't permit us to list them all, but we think they're outstanding.

If you want superb protection for the handwriting area along with some Graffiti-related perks, you're likely to love TapPad.

13

Graffiti Replacements

Love the idea of Graffiti, but don't like Graffiti itself? We understand—some of those special characters are just plain tough (Dave can't make a *j* to save his life, and who can remember the stroke for the percent sign?). Fortunately, you're not stuck with Graffiti—you can write with SimpliWrite instead.

When activated, SimpliWrite supplants Graffiti with its own character set, one that's far more natural. You can dot every "i," cross every "t" and draw a "y" the way it was meant to be drawn. In short, SimpliWrite doesn't limit you to one-stroke characters. Nor does it limit you to the Graffiti area: you can write anywhere on the screen. Wherever you write, SimpliWrite leaves a trail of digital ink, so you can see your characters as you draw them (important for accuracy).

SimpliWrite really shines when it comes to punctuation, banishing Graffiti's cryptic symbols in favor of the real thing. Best of all, some punctuation marks (like the period, comma and "@" sign) don't require you to enter punctuation mode first—just write them as you go.

Our sole complaint with SimpliWrite is that it doesn't offer an automatic capitalization option. Any program designed to simplify data entry should offer "instant capitals" when you write in the middle of the input area. Fortunately, you can use MiddleCaps with it, so problem solved.

Keyboard Replacements

Like to tap-type? Many users prefer the built-in keyboard to Graffiti, if only because it has no real learning curve. Of course, some software developers think they can do the keyboard one better, as evidenced by Textware Solutions' Fitaly Keyboard and a few interesting Hacks.

QWERTY, Meet Fitaly

The Fitaly Keyboard (so named for the layout of its keys, like QWERTY) proceeds from the assumption that the Zire's own built-in keyboard requires too much hand movement. Because it's so wide, you have to move your stylus quite a bit, leading to slow and often inaccurate data entry. The Fitaly Keyboard arranges letters in a tightly knit group designed to minimize stylus travel. Hence, you should be able to tap-type much more quickly.

Clearly, Fitaly represents a radical departure from the standard QWERTY keyboard, and therefore has a high learning curve. Make that practice curve: it could take you several days to master the layout, and even then you might decide you don't like it. The moderate speed gain may not offset the difficulty in learning an entirely new keyboard.

On the other hand, Fitaly is much more practical than the stock built-in keyboard, in part because it makes most common punctuation marks readily available, without the need to shift modes (or even tap the SHIFT key). And when you do access the Numeric mode (done by tapping the 123 button, as with the standard keyboard), you gain access to a number of extended characters (including fractions, the Euro symbol, and more).

Just a Better Keyboard

If you've spent any time with the Zire's standard onscreen keyboard, you've probably been frustrated at having to switch modes to access numbers and punctuation. Horace Ho's Keyboard Hack solves the problem by replacing the standard keyboard with a slightly modified one. His keyboard sports 69 keys, including a numeric keypad and a row of punctuation keys. It also has left/right keys for moving your cursor a space at a time.

13

What About a Real Keyboard?

Whether you use Graffiti or the onscreen keyboard, it won't be as fast for entering data as an actual keyboard. If you want to use your Zire for taking notes, writing sonnets, or anything else that requires a lot of input, check out the Pocketop Keyboard (**www.pocketop.net**).

This handy little accessory folds up so small and thin, it can ride with your Zire in your pocket. Unfolded, it provides a full set of keys—small ones, but acceptable for touch typing. Even more amazing, the Pocketop Keyboard doesn't require a cable or special dock for the Zire—it communicates wirelessly via the Zire's infrared port. Now you just need a decent word-processing program (we recommend Quickword and WordSmith), and your Zire will start looking like a pretty capable laptop replacement. By the way, you may find the Pocketop selling in stores under a different name: Micro Innovations Wireless Link. Same keyboard, different branding.

NOTE
The latter feature, the cursor-control keys, was suggested by a Keyboard Hack user. The author of the program incorporated it into the next version. This is part of what makes the Palm community so great: so many software developers are just regular folks who are happy to hear from regular users.

Give Graffiti a Helping Hand

Remember the old game show *Name That Tune*? The host would describe a song, and the contestant would say, "I can name that tune in three notes." Imagine if Graffiti could adopt that precept, guessing the word or phrase you're writing as you write it. By the time you entered, say, the *e* in "competition," the software would have figured out the rest of the word, thereby saving you six additional pen strokes.

That's the appeal of CIC's WordComplete, a utility that helps you write faster by helping you write less. As you enter characters, a box containing possible word matches appears. If you spy the word you're after, just tap it. The more letters you enter, the closer you get to the correct word (if it's in the software's database).

Obviously, for little words like "the" and "to," the program won't help much, but for longer words, it can indeed save you some scribbling, and WordComplete lets you add your own words and/or short phrases to its database, which can definitely save you time in the long run.

Where to Find It

Web Site	Address	What's There
PalmGear H.Q.	**www.palmgear.com**	MiddleCaps Hack, Clipper, and virtually every other Hack and utility under the sun
Linkesoft	**www.linkesoft.com**	X-Master
Blue Nomad Software	**www.bluenomad.com**	BackupBuddy, WordSmith
Textware Solutions	**www.fitaly.com**	Fitaly Keyboard
Softava	**www.silkyboard.com**	Silkyboard
TapPad	**www.tappad.com**	TapPad
Communications Intelligence Corp.	**www.cic.com**	WordComplete
Horace Ho	**www.horaceho.net**	Keyboard Hack
TealPoint Software	**www.tealpoint.com**	TealEcho

Chapter 14

Problems and Solutions

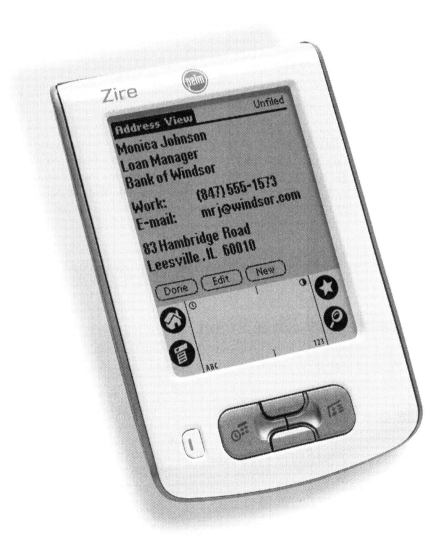

How to...

- Reset your Zire
- Prevent and fix scratched screens
- Fix a screen that no longer responds properly
- Free some extra memory
- Resolve Hack conflicts
- Fix alarms that don't "wake up" your Zire
- Deal with a handheld that suddenly won't HotSync
- Troubleshoot HotSync glitches
- Manage two Zires on one PC
- HotSync one Zire on two PCs
- Find answers to problems on the Web

No computer is perfect. Windows is about as far from the mark as you can get, Macs have problems of their own, and even Zires suffer the occasional meltdown. Usually it's minor: an alarm that fails to "wake up" the unit or a wayward Hack that causes the occasional crash. However, sometimes something downright scary happens, like a sudden and inexplicable lockup that wipes the Zire's entire memory. In this chapter we help you troubleshoot some of the most common Zire maladies and, hopefully, prevent the worst of them.

 *Many common problems are addressed on Palm's Web site. We're not going to rehash them here, but we are going to suggest you check out the site (**www.palm.com/support/**) if you've got a problem we haven't addressed. Chances are good you'll find a solution.*

Cure Zire Problems with a Reset

Just as rebooting a computer will often resolve a glitch or lockup, resetting your Zire is the solution to many a problem. It's usually the first thing you need to do if your Zire crashes—or just acts a little strangely.

Just What Is a "Crash," Anyway?

When a computer crashes, that generally means it has plowed into a brick wall and can no longer function. Fortunately, whereas a car in the same situation would need weeks of bump-and-paint work, a computer can usually return to normal by being rebooted. In the case of Zires, a "reset" is the same as a "reboot."

When a Zire crashes, one common error message is "Fatal Exception." Don't be alarmed; this isn't nearly as morbid as it sounds. It simply means that the Zire has encountered a glitch that proved fatal to its operation. Very often an onscreen Reset button will appear with this error, a tap of which performs a "soft reset" (as we describe in the next section). Sometimes, however, the crash is so fierce that even this button doesn't work. (You know because you tap it and nothing happens.) In a case like that, you have to perform a manual reset.

Different Ways to Reset a Zire

On the back of every Zire, there's a little hole labeled RESET. Hidden inside it is a button that effectively reboots the unit. When that happens, you see the Palm startup screen, followed a few seconds later by the Prefs screen. That's how a successful reset goes. About 98 percent of the time, everything will be as you left it—your data, your applications, everything.

 As you've probably noticed, the RESET hole is pretty small—not even the tip of a pen will fit into it. So, how are you supposed to press the Reset button? The single best tool you can use is a paper clip, though a toothpick will do in a pinch. You can tuck a small paper clip into your wallet and forget about it—until you need it, that is.

Technically speaking, there are three kinds of resets: soft, warm, and hard. (Mind out of the gutter, please.) The details:

- **Soft** Only in rare instances do you need to perform anything other than a soft reset, which is akin to pressing CTRL-ALT-DELETE to reboot your computer. You simply press the Reset button and wait a few seconds while your Zire resets itself. No data is lost.

- **Warm** This action, performed by holding the Scroll-up button while pressing the Reset button, goes an extra step by bypassing any system patches or Hacks you may have installed. Use this only if your Zire fails to respond to a soft reset, meaning it's still locked up, crashing, or stuck in a "boot loop" (the Palm logo is flashing or the screen is displaying garbage). No data is lost, but you have to manually reenable any system patches or Hacks.

- **Hard** With any luck, you'll never have to do this. A hard reset wipes everything out of your Zire's memory, essentially returning it to factory condition. In the exceedingly rare case that your Zire is seriously hosed (meaning it won't reset or even turn off), this should at least get you back to square one. If it doesn't, your handheld is toast and will need to be replaced (more on repair/replacement options later in this chapter). The good news is this: even after a hard reset, all it takes is a HotSync to restore all your data. Some third-party applications may have to be reinstalled manually, but most will just reappear on your handheld. It's like magic!

14

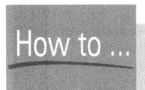 **Perform Warm and Hard Resets**

There's a bit of a trick to doing a warm or hard reset successfully. With your Zire on or off (it doesn't matter), hold down the Scroll-up button (for a warm reset) or the Power button (for a hard reset); then press and release the Reset button on the back of the unit. Now, here's the trick: *wait until the Palm logo appears onscreen* before releasing the Scroll or Power button. If you release both buttons simultaneously, before the logo appears, all you get is a soft reset.

Avoid Battery Problems

Batteries are the lifeblood of any Zire. When they die, they take your data with them, effectively returning your Zire to factory condition. That's why it's vital to keep a close eye on the battery gauge shown at the top of the Applications screen and take heed when the Zire notifies you that your batteries are low.

Of course, if you HotSync regularly, a wiped Zire isn't the end of the world. Once you've recharged the batteries, a HotSync is all it takes to restore virtually everything. Still, there's no reason to let things reach that point. Just make it a habit to plug your Zire into its AC adapter at the end of the day, and you'll never have to worry about running out of juice. If you're taking an extended trip, just toss the AC adapter into your suitcase. A Zire can last several weeks on a single charge, but better safe than sorry.

Fix Scratched Screens

Scratches happen. They happen most often when your stylus hits a piece of dust or grit. That's why it's important to keep your screen as clean as possible (we recommend a daily wipe with a lint-free, antistatic cloth). Better still, take a few preventative steps:

- **Tape** A piece of Scotch Magic Tape 811 placed over the Graffiti input area (where most scratches occur) not only makes existing scratches less tangible while you're writing, but also prevents future scratches and provides a tackier writing surface.

- **Screen protection sheets** Incipio Screen Protectors are plastic overlays that protect the entire screen. They won't remove scratches, but they will prevent them and, like the tape, make them less pronounced. If you visit **www.freescreenprotectors.com**, you can get a package of 12 for just $6.95 shipped (enter coupon code FREESP during checkout).

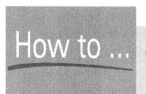 **Cure "Mad Digitizer Syndrome"**

What happens when the digitizer gets so out of whack that your Zire essentially becomes inoperable? This problem, which some have dubbed "Mad Digitizer Syndrome," tends to plague older models, though it can strike even if your handheld is only a year or two old. One very effective way to cure MDS is with a utility called AutoDigi, which automatically recalibrates the digitizer after a reset. You can buy the $15 program at PalmGear (**www.palmgear.com**). If your screen is really giving you trouble, check out OnDigi, a Hack that automatically recalibrates the digitizer each time you turn on your handheld.

Fix a Screen That No Longer Responds Properly

As noted in Chapter 2's discussion of the Digitizer option, it's not uncommon to experience some "drift" in the screen's response to your stylus taps. An example: you have to tap just a bit to the left or right of your desired target for the tap to be recognized. This occurs over time, when the accuracy of the digitizer (the hardware that makes the screen respond to your input) degrades.

Unless the digitizer has gotten so off-kilter that you can no longer operate your Zire, the solution is to hit the Prefs icon and choose Digitizer from the right-corner menu. Here you can reset the digitizer, effectively making your Palm good as new. If you can't even manage to tap Prefs, you can do a soft reset (as described earlier in this chapter). That gets you to the Prefs screen, where you should at least be able to select the Digitizer option.

Reclaim Memory for Software and Data

A common problem among Zire users—especially those who discover games and e-books—is running out of memory. If you suddenly find yourself in a memory crunch and need space for something important (say, a work-related spreadsheet), you need to do a little housekeeping and clear a little space.

14

Solving Memory-Related HotSync Failure

If you try to install a new program or database and your Zire doesn't have enough memory, the HotSync will fail—and fail again every time thereafter. Assuming you can't free up enough space on your handheld to accommodate the new item(s), you have to venture onto your hard drive. Specifically, locate the *c:\program files\palm\yourusername\install* folder (the "holding tank" for software waiting to be installed during HotSync) and delete everything that's in there. Now you should be able to HotSync successfully.

 *Deleting programs and data from the Install folder doesn't permanently delete them from your hard drive. When you choose items to be installed on your Zire, copies are placed in the Install folder. The original files remain.*

How to Delete

To delete software from your Zire, tap the Applications button and choose Menu | App | Delete.

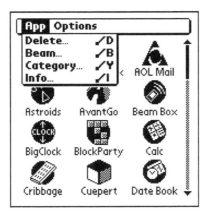

In a few seconds, you see a list of all the applications, utilities, games, and so on installed on your Zire. What you won't find here are e-books, Doc files, image files, individual spreadsheets, and other kinds of data. For items like those, you need to use their respective applications to delete them. Say you imported some spreadsheets into Quicksheet or some e-books into Palm Reader— the only way to delete those documents is from within the two programs.

As you can see, the Delete screen tells you the size of each item, so you know just how much space you free up with each deletion. To remove something, just tap it to highlight it and tap Delete.

What To Delete

Don't bother culling through your contact list or appointment calendar. Though they may be large, deleting a handful of entries will have a negligible impact on the Zire's total memory. Programs, on the other hand, can add up quickly. Here's a list of items to consider ditching:

- ■ **Games**   Although many of them are relatively small, some, like SimCity, can eat up a pretty large chunk of memory. If you don't play it anymore, or can live without it for a while, ditch it.

- ■ **E-books**   No sense keeping books you've already read, especially if they occupy several hundred kilobytes of RAM.

- ■ **Data files**   Spreadsheets, Doc files, and databases can be quite large. Eliminate the ones you no longer need.

Resolve Hack Conflicts

It bears repeating (see Chapter 13 for the first time we said it) that as marvelous as Hacks are, they can occasionally wreak havoc on Zires. This is especially true if you run more than two or three simultaneously, as these little bits of code can conflict with one another. If you find that your Zire is crashing on a regular basis, you may have to investigate your Hacks. Here's what you should do:

1. Start X-Master; then uncheck the box next to each Hack to disable it.

2. Go back to using your Zire. If you find that the crashes no longer occur, a Hack is the likely culprit. To help pin down which one, go on to step 3.

3. Launch X-Master again and enable just one Hack. Use your Zire normally and see if the crashes return. If not, enable a second Hack. Through this process of elimination, you should be able to figure out which one is causing the problem. When you do, stop using it.

14

Fix a Zire that Won't "Wake Up" for Alarms

It's easy to fall out of love with your Zire when an alarm you set fails to go off (meaning the Zire doesn't "wake up" and beep). There are several reasons this can happen, from low batteries to a corrupted alarm database to a conflict with third-party software. The first is easy to resolve by making sure your Zire is adequately charged. For the other two problems, try a soft reset, which very often does the trick.

If you use a third-party program that has anything to do with alarms (such as ToDo Plus, DiddleBug, and so forth), it's very possible this is causing the snafu. To troubleshoot it, try doing a warm reset (hold the Scroll-up button while pressing the Reset button). This will disable any Hacks or third-party applications that tie into the operating system. Set an alarm in Date Book and see if it works. If so, then another program is very likely to blame. A process of elimination should help you determine which one. In any case, you may to have discontinue using that program if it keeps fouling up your alarms.

If none of these options work, it's possible your Zire is damaged. Contact Palm for service.

Beaming Problems

Having trouble beaming? Chances are good the problem is caused by one of three factors. First, make sure the two handhelds aren't too close together. People often make the mistake of holding their Zires right next to each other, which can give the infrared transceivers trouble. Keep the units at least a foot or two apart (their range is about five feet).

Second, make sure the Beam Receive option is checked in the Prefs | General screen. While you may not have unchecked it yourself, sometimes it just seems to happen.

If neither of these suggestions solves the problem, try moving to a darker area. Beaming doesn't always work if you're in a brightly lit room or outdoors on a sunny day.

If all else fails, you might want to perform a soft reset on both Zires; that might clear up a problem that was keeping your devices from chatting with each other.

The Last Chapter

Dave: Well, this is the last chapter…and it's almost complete. It was a blast to write this book, but I have to admit that I'm a kind of burnt out on all this tech writing stuff. I think I'll take my half of the advance (a cool half-million or so) and move to Bermuda. There, I'll build a cottage on the beach and let my army of trained monkey butlers bring me cool drinks all day long. I'll pass the time staring at the waves as they gently break onto the sandy, white beach, and occasionally dabble at writing a best-selling novel on my Zire whenever I'm not scuba diving in the shimmering blue sea. My MP3 player will be loaded up with Kristin Hersh music, and my cats will be napping in my lap. Yep, that's what I'm going to do…

Rick: Always with the monkey butlers. As for me, now that the yoke of another book has been lifted, I'll be returning to the soup kitchen where I volunteer three times a week, though not before I finish the urban-beautification program I spearheaded and the fundraiser for Greenpeace. Just have to decide which charities will be getting my royalty checks this year—always a tough choice. Honestly, there's no better reward for months of hard work than good old philanthropy. Oh, but, uh, your plan sounds really good too…

Troublesome USB Ports

All Zires rely on the Universal Serial Bus (USB) for connecting to a PC. While USB ports are generally problem-free, problems can arise. Here are a few thoughts to consider if you're having HotSync troubles:

- On a Windows-based PC, USB is guaranteed to work only with Windows 98 or higher. If you still have Windows 95, get with the program——upgrade if you expect to reliably use USB devices like the Zire.

- If HotSyncs sometimes fail to work, you might have too many USB devices connected to a single USB port. Move the Zire cable to another USB port. You might need a powered USB hub, as there may not be enough juice in the port to supply power to all the devices you have connected.

- Check the Palm and Microsoft Windows Web sites for more USB troubleshooting information.

Deal with a Zire that Will No Longer HotSync

It worked fine yesterday, but today your handheld just refuses to HotSync. We hear your pain—this drives us up the wall, too. We wish we could blame Windows, because it's just the kind of nonsense we've come to expect from it, but this is usually due to a Zire software, hardware, or cable problem.

Best bet? Start with a soft reset. Use the end of a paper clip (or unscrew the barrel of your metal stylus to find a hidden tip) to press the Reset button on the back of your handheld. In many cases, this will solve the problem outright, and you can get back to playing Bejeweled. If it doesn't, consider reinstalling Palm Desktop. This action won't affect your data, but it will provide a "fresh" version of HotSync Manager—which often solves HotSync problems. If you're not comfortable with that step or it doesn't work, consult Palm's Web site for other remedies.

14

Solve the Most Common HotSync Problems

There are just a few pesky problems that account for about 90 percent of all the HotSync issues we've ever encountered—and they're all pretty easy to diagnose and solve.

The Zire Aborts a HotSync Immediately

If you tap the HotSync icon and the Zire immediately insists that the COM port is in use—so fast that it doesn't seem possible for the Zire to have checked—the solution is to perform a soft reset. After that, it should HotSync normally.

When HotSyncing, the Zire Displays the HotSync Screen, but Absolutely Nothing Else Happens

Frequently, this problem is just a result of one of the HotSync dialog boxes being open. If, for instance, you open the Custom option to change conduit settings, the HotSync will not run and you won't get an error message—so look on the desktop for an open dialog box and close it.

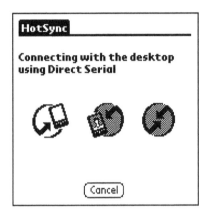

When HotSyncing, This Message Appears: "An application failed to respond to a HotSync"

This one is easy to fix. When you started the HotSync, an Address Book or Date Book entry was probably left open in Palm Desktop. Your Zire can't successfully HotSync with one of those entries open for editing, so you should close the entry and try again.

Outlook HotSync Problems

As you learned in Chapter 3, most Zires come with a special conduit for synchronizing with Microsoft Outlook. It's called PocketMirror, and we could fill a separate book with information on using and troubleshooting it. Fortunately, you can get lots of helpful assistance from Chapura, the company that makes it (**www.chapura.com**).

Working with Windows XP

Palm Desktop doesn't support Windows XP's "switch user" option, which allows multiple users to log onto their PCs at the same time. If you have multiple user profiles set up, each person needs to log out at the end of their session, while the next person logs in.

Also, if you upgrade your PC from an earlier version of Windows to Windows XP, it will probably be necessary to reinstall the Palm Desktop software. That's because the upgrade can mess up the Zire's USB driver. Fortunately, reinstalling Palm Desktop is no big deal—it won't erase any of your data and shouldn't cause a single wrinkle.

Manage Multiple Zires or PCs

The Palm OS allows you to HotSync the same Zire to more than one PC or to HotSync several Zires to the same PC. Trust us when we say it's both safe and easy—so long as you adhere to a few guidelines. Rick, for example, has three different handhelds connected to his computer—and one of them isn't even a Palm!

Two Handhelds on a Single PC

Given the Zire's low price, it wouldn't be all that unusual for each member of your family to own one, but what if you have only one computer? Not a problem, as long as each Zire has a unique HotSync ID—the name you give it the very first time you HotSync (see Chapter 3). Assuming that's the case, you can synchronize two, three, four, or really any number of Zires to a single PC, and each person's data will be kept separate. Imagine your PC as a file cabinet with X number of drawers, and each Zire owner gets his or her own drawer.

What if you have a Zire and your spouse has, say, a Palm m515? The same HotSync ID rule applies: as long as they're different, you should have no trouble synchronizing them to the same PC.

Adding a Second Zire

So you just bought your spouse a shiny new Zire, and now you're ready to HotSync it to your PC for the first time. The process is the same: just plug in the HotSync cradle; then tap the Star icon. Because it's the first time, HotSync Manager will display a box asking you to select a user (you should see the first Zire's HotSync ID). Click the New button and type in whatever HotSync ID you want for the new Zire.

Make absolutely sure you choose a different HotSync ID. If two Zires have the same ID and you sync them to the same PC, havoc will ensue. Can't remember your own HotSync ID? Well, you just saw it listed in that dialog box, but you can also look it up right on your Zire. Tap the HotSync icon (the one in the Applications screen, not the Star icon) and look in the upper-right corner. Your HotSync ID appears there.

Two PCs for a Single Zire

The Zire can keep two different PCs straight just as easily as one PC can keep a pair of Zires straight. When you HotSync, the Zire updates the second PC with whatever data it previously got from the first PC, and vice versa. This is a great way to keep your office PC and home computer in sync, or even a PC and a Mac—the Zire can serve as a nonpartisan conduit for keeping all the data in agreement.

While not essential, we recommend making sure that you have the same version of the Palm Desktop on both PCs. If you're using a PC and a Mac, you can't do that, but you should keep up with the latest release of the Palm Desktop for Macintosh.

14

Of course, the most efficient way to use a dual-PC system is to acquire a second HotSync cable. Palm offers a Zire Travel Kit that includes not only a spare cable, but also another charger. It's available from Palm's Web site for $24.95.

Where to Find Help

Palm's Web site is obviously the best place to start for any Zire-related problems. However, you may also want to visit some independent Web sites that offer tips, tricks, hints, and technical solutions. If you're looking for answers that aren't in this book or on the Palm site, try some of these.

Site	Description
www.palmgear.com	Look for both the Tips & Tricks section and Calvin's FAQ.
www.pdabuzz.com	This site has a message board area in which you can post questions and read answers to common questions. It also contains Palm-related product news and reviews.
alt.comp.sys.palmtops.pilot comp.sys.palmtops.pilot	These newsgroups are available to anyone with a newsreader like Outlook Express. They are threaded message boards that contain questions and answers about Palm issues. You can post your own questions, respond to what's already there, or just read the existing posts.

Index

INTERNATIONAL CONTACT INFORMATION

AUSTRALIA
McGraw-Hill Book Company Australia Pty. Ltd.
TEL +61-2-9900-1800
FAX +61-2-9878-8881
http://www.mcgraw-hill.com.au
books-it_sydney@mcgraw-hill.com

CANADA
McGraw-Hill Ryerson Ltd.
TEL +905-430-5000
FAX +905-430-5020
http://www.mcgraw-hill.ca

GREECE, MIDDLE EAST, & AFRICA
(Excluding South Africa)
McGraw-Hill Hellas
TEL +30-210-6560-990
TEL +30-210-6560-993
TEL +30-210-6560-994
FAX +30-210-6545-525

MEXICO (Also serving Latin America)
McGraw-Hill Interamericana Editores S.A. de C.V.
TEL +525-117-1583
FAX +525-117-1589
http://www.mcgraw-hill.com.mx
fernando_castellanos@mcgraw-hill.com

SINGAPORE (Serving Asia)
McGraw-Hill Book Company
TEL +65-863-1580
FAX +65-862-3354
http://www.mcgraw-hill.com.sg
mghasia@mcgraw-hill.com

SOUTH AFRICA
McGraw-Hill South Africa
TEL +27-11-622-7512
FAX +27-11-622-9045
robyn_swanepoel@mcgraw-hill.com

SPAIN
McGraw-Hill/Interamericana de España, S.A.U.
TEL +34-91-180-3000
FAX +34-91-372-8513
http://www.mcgraw-hill.es
professional@mcgraw-hill.es

UNITED KINGDOM, NORTHERN,
EASTERN, & CENTRAL EUROPE
McGraw-Hill Education Europe
TEL +44-1-628-502500
FAX +44-1-628-770224
http://www.mcgraw-hill.co.uk
computing_europe@mcgraw-hill.com

ALL OTHER INQUIRIES Contact:
Osborne/McGraw-Hill
TEL +1-510-549-6600
FAX +1-510-883-7600
http://www.osborne.com
omg_international@mcgraw-hill.com

New Offerings from Osborne's
How to Do Everything Series

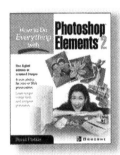

www.ingramcontent.com/pod-product-compliance
Lightning Source LLC
Chambersburg PA
CBHW080405060326
40689CB00019B/4144